DAVID BOWIE

— THE STARZONE INTERVIEWS —

Edited by David Currie

Text: David Currie/Kevin Cann   Design: Gina Coyle

Omnibus Press
London/New York/Sydney/Cologne

© Copyright 1985 Omnibus Press
(A Division of Book Sales Limited)

Edited by David Currie.
Picture research by David Currie.
Cover painting and book design by Gina Coyle.

Angie Bowie, Visconti, Mayes, Slick, Kemp, Simms and Roeg interviews
conducted and written by David Currie.

Pitt, Kornilof, Ronson, Gillespie, Lower Third and Hutchinson interviews
conducted and written by Kevin Cann.

ISBN No. 0.7119.0685
Order No. OP43355

Exclusive distributors:
Book Sales Limited
78 Newman Street, London W1P 3LA, UK.
Cherry Lane Books
PO Box 430, Port Chester, NY 10573, USA.
Omnibus Press
GPO Box 3304, Sydney, NSW 2001, Australia.

To the Music Trade only:
Music Sales Limited
78 Newman Street, London W1P 3LA, UK.

Typeset by Admin Watford Limited
Printed in England by Ebenezer Baylis & Son Limited

C o n t e n t s

The interviews contained in this volume were conducted from the middle of 1983 to the beginning of 1985 and originally published in abridged form in 'Starzone', the magazine of David Bowie.

The years we spent working on 'Starzone' gave ourselves and, we hope, a lot of other people a great deal of fun, interest and a positive channelling of our damnable admiration for this inscrutable man!

Whilst dedications are somewhat superfluous in books of this nature – Thanks are duly extended to all those who not only gave unselfishly of their time but also of their private recollections to make this book possible . . .

4

Firstword

It's become common practice for serious biographers to expand the depth of their work by talking to as many people as possible associated with the subject matter.

Those with somewhat tenuous links are usually relegated to the one-liner league, but equally, and much more importantly, those with far more involved connections are also denied the opportunity to fully reflect on the worth, or lack thereof, of their working relationships with whomever it is the biographer is researching.

Due to a much acclaimed and much dissected artistic career, David Bowie has inspired a vast and often barren assortment of books aiming to chart his life in simple biographical fashion.

Such is the price of monumental fame to attract such attention, where the barest anecdote and single scribbled word is savoured by devotees with perhaps a little more relish than is palatable.

It can't be denied by those with more than a passing interest in popular music that Bowie's recorded and thespian output is of sufficient substance to warrant close inspection – but between the clipped quotes and analytical copy, the repeated chain events and facts, some sight is often lost of the human being behind the masks.

The approach that this book has taken is to avoid any history lessons and truth-searching essays but to indulge, with a good deal of background knowledge, in informal conversations with key figures that have, throughout each period of his career, worked closely with David Bowie.

On such a level it becomes clearer to understand his working methods, and far simpler to arrive at some kind of conclusion about what this highly gifted man is really like.

Viewed not as some rock avatar with electric bolts of concentrated genius emanating from every move, but as a talented artist working to define the barriers of ability.

No single book will ever provide the 'definitive' story of the life of such an individual as David Bowie. An autobiography would be fun, but if Bowie's often dismissive attitude towards his own work is anything to go by, then hardly a treasure-trove of seriousness.

Above all, David Bowie is a private person, with good reason and good sense. This collection of opinion, impression and memory will, at least, enable those with an interest strong enough to peek behind doors that were previously closed very tightly indeed.

David Currie, Spring 1985

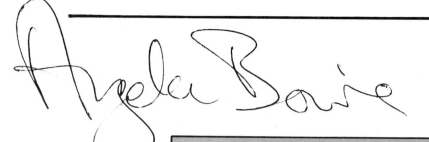

Angela Bowie – Occurring Incidents

A pool of electric energy that charged the spirit of outrageousness in the early to mid-70's, lighting the spark to the Bowie media flame, glowering eyes that leapt and danced to attentive observers and quite often re-charging the creative batteries of the other Bowie, with whom she shared her love, his fame and their dreams.

When all was calm and steady, the Bowies conceived a public marriage, a loose and amicable affair that exalted the virtues of love (per se), and lived a life of artistry on a level which shocked many, baffled most and thrilled all. The multi-sexual Bowies. Both boyish, both girlish. Both wildly colourful, dangerously seductive, creatures that had seemingly leapt from the canvas of some highly imaginative painter or had floated to earth from some glittering planet in a nether region of space.

Together, apart, they were one. David was Ziggy and Angie was Ziggy's mate.

The pursuits of sexual liberty that they both strongly upheld and encouraged, the gay marriage, the proclamation of love for all by all, and the wholly unpredictable flavour helped wipe out the naïvety of the permissive 60's and opened up the fabric of young love in a manner that angered as many as it pleased. The Bowies, those strange and alien space-faces, were as feared as they were loved.

Then it all went wrong. As gay people furthered the cause to lift the taboo against public acceptance or tolerance of homosexuality, the ideas and dreams that created this marriage made in Mars became tarnished and unfulfilled.

David and Angela drifted apart as fame, the angry beast that it is, demanded more and more attention. The divorce was final and uncluttered by romantic notions of a world where love is all.

The parting was sweet and sour. Each was reluctant to throw any substantial blame. It seemed, quite simply, that the flame had flickered out rather than been blown out in a fit of antagonism.

The child, Zowie Bowie, now known more sedately as Joey Bowie, remains the only tangible link between the two ex-partners and those heady, exuberant days.

While both have matured and outgrown the gritted teeth defiance of youth, the saddest part of the Bowie fable is that these two people no longer have a clear line of communication.

If any bitterness towards David remains on Angela's part, there was no evidence of it when I talked to her early in 1985...

♦ *A marriage made in Mars*

Kentish Times

♦ *A local reporter is to thank for these photographs of the Bowie wedding day, March 20, 1970.*

b o w

SHE STILL looked a million dollars. The hair was swept back, up from her angular face, jagged, bright blonde and punkette. The dancer's figure, poured into a skin-tight leopard cat-suit, was still lithe and stylistically thin. Accompanied by prepared tapes, she energetically performed a 20-minute set of sultry, pounding music – her movements precise and agile. One couldn't help, with that mop of spiked hair, flashes of crimson make-up and finely-sculptured face, to be reminded of a less awkward Ziggy Stardust. Angela Bowie was on stage at Planet X night club in Liverpool – a club situated in historic Matthew Street where once stood The Cavern in the heyday of The Beatles and Mersey-Beat, vandalised now during an act of civic stupidity. Crowded tightly around the barrier at the front of the stage, a horde of Bat-Cave scousers eyed the proceedings with interest. Only occasionally, during the performance of a poem called 'SUCK-cess' would the odd remark like 'We know who that's about' rise from the audience. Reaction was subdued yet affectionately favourable. Angie smiled a lot and so did we.

Back-stage at Planet X, in the spacious and somewhat makeshift dressing room, another crowd had assembled. Friends of ours through the magazine, friends and general helpers of Angie's and patrons of the club who just wandered in to ogle the ex-wife of a superstar, perhaps ask a question or two and snatch an autograph.

This woman, Angela, is a bundle of activity. The arms and eyes became a theatre of their own. She talked eagerly and excitedly and what follows is not dissimilar to a free-fall crescendo of questions, answers and occurring incidents . . .

"The reason it's taken so long for me to come back and perform," said Angie, "is because I've been working a lot in America. It's a big place and you kind of get stuck there. I guess I really wanted to make sure that I was good before I came to England. The reaction in the States was fantastic, so I feel it's time that I did it all. I'm too much of an Anglophile to do everything in the States. I'm contracted to finish an album in London, which makes me very happy. I've already recorded six tracks in America, so I'm pleased that it's weighted on both sides. I only really lived in the States over the past four years, running my horse ranch in California. I went to college in London so it's home much more to me. I'm still a bit of a wal in America – It

doesn't mean that much to me."

Recent work for Angela Bowie includes early live performances in New York and an extensive tour of the West Coast of America where she was supported musically by a band comprising 'much desired' musicians who collectively go by the name of Candy, and are described by Angie as 'a bunch of healthy Keith Richards '. Musical collaborator Chico Ray is a permanent fixture and there is talk of Earl Slick (a very accomplished guitarist who also has a far-reaching track record with the other Bowie) joining Angie's touring band. The obvious question opened the interview proper:

Are you fearful of any bad press for retaining the Bowie name?

"No, if you're frightened of the press they pick on you. I really like the press as the English press gave me my first break when I was modelling fashion clothes, so I try to work with them. I'm also very fortunate because I have never been misquoted – I always said things that were outrageous anyway, so no-one ever needed to re-write anything! To be fearful of press would cause untold angst. It's like saying, was I fearful of David telling the press he was bi-sexual which got him the front cover of Melody Maker? We'd only been trying to get that for a year and a half! As far as the name goes – I don't have any choice. Every time I've tried to change my name, no one will call me by the new one (laughs). I've tried three times and no-one will listen to me – 'Jipp Jones?', they'll say 'Naah, you're Angie Bowie'. There was a poster for one of my gigs I saw the other day that read 'Ex-Mrs David Bowie'! There's really nothing I can do about it. I helped make that name famous, anyway."

You mentioned that the first of your poems 'Soul House' to be set to music was a collaboration with Roy Martin. Did David ever work with you on anything?

"No. We were too busy. We used to mess around with things late at night and I felt really honoured when some tunes would have things in them that we had talked about together. But David always re-wrote it so it was his own work. I was very young and I never worried about things like that, which was totally right. I mean, where else could you get a university seminar in rock and roll working with somebody so fabulous. I think we got closer to working together when we were in New York. I've always been heavily into visuals and video so I wasn't that

Final Bowie
It's all over with Angie says David

From KENELM JENOU
In Cannes
mad marriage of
id Bowie a
ally
ale
g
f

Outrageous

" Naturally we bo
access to our s

of

the bizarre Bowies.
how and
g the second ha

STARBURST: End

otal
owie
"
build
s, re-
arlier

oncert
urprise
love to

trousers
ning of
kin coat
e said.

concerned about putting music to my poetry; my concern was that whatever David did was on film or video and that's when I worked hardest with him. In New York we worked a lot on a Diamond Dogs video. The entire suite of the Pierre Hotel built into a model of the Diamond Dogs city and we micro-videoed it. It was full of these little odd people and the sets were all made and painted by David, he's a fabulous painter. You know those old **Gerry Anderson** puppet shows, it was like that. So we filmed this marvellously weird city, zooming in with these micro/macro cameras – the whole thing was puppets and rocket-ships. **Iggy** was with us and David wanted him to star in the video. David would direct, and I wrote some dialogue. That was great fun and probably the most involved collaboration we ever did. You can imagine, David was doing so many things and had so many projects back to back that the only thing that would make me panic is that he might become so exhausted that he wouldn't be able to finish his work. I worried a lot about his health. That was the only thing I was crazy about because he had this great capacity for work. He never did when I first met him – **Tony Visconti** would always say that David was totally un-centred, that he never followed projects through and that was true in a way because he has a grasshopper mind. Together it was fantastic because I could keep his interest up, keep feeding him and make him finish a project. He became a fabulous, but dangerous to his health, workaholic. From someone who was flighty to someone who literally kept going until the work was done. As I said, the only detrimental aspect was that he might become ill and I worried a lot about that."

Was he encouraging of your own creativity?

"He encouraged me as long as it was in relation to what we were doing, not because he wasn't an inspiration to other people's talents but because there were only 24 hours in a day. David would live three or four days awake and then rest for two days and I tried to explain to him that you don't end up with more time awake because the last day you're so exhausted and not as bright as you would be if you had kept proper sleeping hours. There were so many commitments. The more we made people aware of the importance of video and film, all we were doing was making our own workload worse. 'What a great idea!', they would say, 'Do it!' – So we were kind of cutting off our noses to spite our faces. It just got crazier for us."

When you formulated your marriage agreement...

"Oh, darling, **Don Short** vowed. He drew up that little thing. *(Don Short was the literary editor of Angie's memoirs 'Free Spirit'. The book stated that David and Angie 'Vowed that infidelity would never threaten our marriage. Vowed that we would never give way to possessiveness. Vowed that we would never harbour secrets from each other. Vowed that we would remain together forever and that no-one would infringe our commitment"!)* . We never formulated

♦ *Take one*

anything. David asked me to marry him and I said OK. I kept getting sent out of the country. David's no fool, he realised that every time I got sent out of the country he got two weeks behind. He was also still pining for **Hermione Farthingale,** he really was. He wanted to slap her in the face with one hand and make sure that I stayed in the country with the other. Another thing was that David always loved playing with children so I said to him, 'Why don't you have your own? You could play with your own child. It really might be a good idea'. He thought about that for a couple of months and decided that he liked that idea. So then it started to become like a real marriage. We never really

considered it was a real marriage apart from the fact it was lovely to have a child, we both are very responsible people with children. Then everyone thought that we were outrageous because of the way we talked, but we had never changed. It only looked like a marriage because there was a mother, a father and a child. There was this nuclear family. (laughs).

I think it's always difficult when artists live together, to allow the leniency. You must take things with a pinch of salt and not worry about how other people live."

What do you remember about Haddon Hall? – That was your first real home with David.

♦ *Take two*

"Well, I basically organised everyone. You have to understand, I was the head girl at my school in Switzerland, I can organise anyone to do anything. I'm an organisational genius. So at 11.30 it was UP! Breakfast. Shirts ironed, who's got meetings where? Cars leaving at 1.30, you're going with him, you're going with her, David, you're staying home to write, I'm going out.... (*Angie shouts the above in a broad Cockney accent. Throughout the interview, her dialect would veer from Americanese through to English proper and rampant Cockney. An unaffected and entertaining trait.*)

"We were there for a long time, the band came down from Hull, Tony Visconti moved in with his girlfriend – he eventually moved back into town because he was doing so much work with **Marc Bolan.** When the traffic's bad from Beckenham, darling, you're talking about an hour each way. He bought himself a motorbike, zipped back and forth so it was much easier for him.

I felt better for having them all around me. First of all I could keep track of them and the writing came together much quicker. Also, I'd promised Mrs. Ronson that I wouldn't let anything happen to them. God knows they were wild on the road but at least at home I could look after them. But it was good. Good times. It was big enough for everyone's ego."

That was important?

"Well, nobody had a problem with it. I was amazed. Everyone lived in great harmony. It was a lot easier when you have a head girl. No-one ever told anyone what to do. It was just scheduling and no-one gets cross about things like that. I have boundless energy, and I was lucky because when they were carrying on at 10.30 I was out like a light so I could get up in the morning and deal with it all."

Would David ask opinions when he had just written a song?

"Of course he did. Not just me, the band, the band's girlfriends, people downstairs just passing (laughs). You know, it's so fabulous to try out new songs on people. I know I do. As soon as Chico and I have finished a song we round everyone up – 'Right! Seddown! Listen to this! You don't like it? What are you – Stoopid!! (laughs) All that good stuff...."

'Before you carry on' came a voice from behind a video camera, Graham McDougall video buff and friend of the magazine. 'Can I just ask what happened to the Diamond Dogs video?'

"What do you think?, *replied Angie,* David's sitting on it. He's a collector. He's got all my videos, all his videos. Everything! I made sure that he kept copies. All the rehearsals from the Ziggy and Diamond Dogs tours. Most are in black and white but some are in colour. Just tripod video. I couldn't comment on the quality, I'd have to see them all again because I'm so involved with video now my judgement is better."

The conversation seemed fixed, for the moment, on video, so Angie continued to explain her own video dabblings:

"This whole thing that I'm doing now is as a video artist. I make music because I want soundtracks for my videos. The music's real important, but I'm more a video artist than a recording artist. It's taken four years to explain that to recording companies but they're beginning to understand.

When we got divorced I could have argued about it but I didn't. David's the kind of person that when something's finished, it's finished. I didn't argue about my son so I wasn't going to argue about videos. I argued about things that I knew he didn't really care about, like my Persian rugs and my art collection.

He was having a nervous breakdown and I didn't want to make things worse for him. I really didn't. He was a sick puppy that year. You know, when you love someone you get so into where their head's at that no matter

11

RCA

what someone's filtering into their mind or what they're saying as a result of what they feel, it's like water off a duck's back. I just wanted to leave him in peace. It's hard enough to maintain sanity without having someone who you think loves you making a fuss over stuff like that. I'm a bit like David in a way, I can't go backwards.

And the other thing is, there's a situation of power-play. And the power-play is if there's anything that I wanted, then that would be a reason for **Corinne Schwab** to make damn sure I didn't get it.

David knows I care because I talk about David the same way I've always talked about him which is with great admiration. Forget about all the love, but with great respect for him as an artist. I had the great pleasure and joy of working with him. He really turned me on to how much an artist can achieve in so many different areas. People always used to say 'David, you've got to stick to this' and I used to reply 'No, he doesn't. He doesn't have to stick to music. He can do whatever the hell he wants.' That's the privilege of being an artist. And so it works in both of those areas. I can't allow myself to be weak. When I was 7 years old, I was at school in Cyprus and I had

long, blonde ringlets. In my school there were 23 boys and four girls. They put lizards in my hair and when lizards are frightened they drop their tails. So even when I managed to get the lizards out I couldn't get the tails out.

I went home to my dad, scared out of my wits, it was the most terrible experience. My father, who was a colonel and a war hero, really despised weakness, said 'Play with lizards. Don't tell me how ugly it was.' So I played with lizards until I knew the next time someone came up to me with a creepy crawly I'd go: 'Tarantula? Does he bite? He doesn't bite if he's in a good mood, right? Cute.'

The experience with the lizards was terrible but it's probably one of the best things that ever happened to me because I knew I'd never let things get to me in that way ever again.

I can't really talk about why Corinne is still with David. But whatever makes a person happy is fine by me. I think she's a witch, but that's my opinion, it's not his. And if it makes him happy then I'm delighted. Because it's very lonely at the top and I've seen David very lonely and I didn't like it. I'll tell you one thing, no way is she having an easy time because David isn't an easy person to live

with. Not if your heart is with him. And David always knew that I protected myself from him. I adored him but it was over there. If I needed to sleep with him every night I'd have been a very lonely girl. To the point where David thought that I didn't care, but I did, it's just that I can't show any weakness."

Do you still have an interest in his work?

"No. The last thing I had an interest in was 'Blue Jean' – I actually sent him a telegram and told him how wonderful it was. I think the last four albums were horrible, miserable, uncreative and very boring. For David to be boring is something. I suppose in a hundred years' time, if they remember any of us in rock and roll, they'll refer to that as his blue period, if you want to look at it on a 30 album scale. But I didn't like them. I didn't actually like the song 'Blue Jean' but I cared for the fact that he had bothered to make the video, that made me feel real happy. David's films I love, but I don't watch those either because they upset me.

When he looks strained or tired, even though it's only acting, I know him too well. I understand every thought that goes in and goes out of his head. I've seen David when he really was tired and upset, so why put yourself through things that bother you? Every time he looked haggard or worried it made my stomach churn over."

Did you ever receive any comment from David on your book?

"Are you kidding? It's the nicest book in the world. What could he say? 'I hope you made lots of money'? No, I haven't spoken to David properly for eight years. We talk briefly at Christmas."

How often do you see Joey?

"We see each other all the time. He comes to me for the holidays. But we don't talk about his dad, he's in a difficult situation and I don't like to make things worse. It doesn't really bother me – If it did, I'd be a fool to myself.

I've been screaming for years that all I wanted was the chance to do what I can do, so if I'm going to sit around moping it wouldn't help anything.

The only thing that I am prone to do from time to time is yell at the radio. David is a Yorkshireman and he's very tight with money. Never was with me, he was always over-generous, he was divine. But a couple of albums after 'Young Americans' there'd be huge songs that were like phone calls to me from David but he didn't want to pay the

Mick Rock

phone bill. So let the record company put it out and I'll hear it on the radio."

(This recalls a scene from 'The Man Who Fell to Earth' which David had just completed filming during the period that Angie indicates. Thomas Jerome Newton, the stranded alien, makes a record in his alien tongue, intended for his wife on his home planet which would one day pick up the radio frequency from Earth. 'We hear most things on the radio these days.')

"So at certain stages, I'd be talking to someone and suddenly start yelling at the radio; 'Stop! Don't interrupt!' They all thought I was nuts. (laughs). That happens quite a lot. So in that way, I'm always aware of him. I think we watch over each other."

What does Joey remember of the early days?

"Not much probably. I don't really know. He probably has flashes of things that he liked, but that would be things like Disneyland or whatever. Endless car rides definitely. We took him to some of the Ziggy shows, especially in America because we didn't want to leave him at home. He's a very creative boy.

I was extremely happy when I watched him with 'Dungeons and Dragons', watched him develop entire scripts and characters and draw up all the maps. I was very pleased. A lot of his father in him, it's very good. For a while there I was scared he was going to be a bank manager because his favourite toys were calculators and computers and I thought 'What have we got going on here?' (laughs). But he's very creative. That makes you feel good, to see your kids like that."

You have a daughter as well...

"Yes, **Stasia** *(Laranna Celeste)*. She's four and a half. Never mind about that one. I'm terrified of her. By the time she's sixteen I think she'll probably rule the world. Or the male population at least. She's heavy duty. She's amazing. That's Zowie's favourite person in the world."

Do you still have your wedding bracelets?

(Displays two golden bracelets around her left wrist). "These aren't the originals but they're from the same bunch. My mother died last year. I wear these so I do in a way, but it's just being married to memories, which is good, otherwise you tend to forget where you came from and those wedding bracelets remind me of where I came from."

During press conferences in 1983 David

wore two bracelets on his left hand. Does he retain the originals?

"Very probably. I really have no way of knowing. I'm delighted he wears them. He should do. David's got a mind like mine which is pretty much like a rabbit warren. I'll tell you a funny thing about getting older – The memory banks get full. I'll search for a name and as a youngster it would come to me maybe a phrase later but now it takes me much longer. And I thought it was because I was getting old, but then I realised it was clogged memory banks. There's so much stuff in there it takes the computer that much longer to dig up the information. So, I think in a lot of ways, you block off things you don't want to think about because it hurts. But if you really wanted to, you could unseal the doors and get in there. And, if they are the same bracelets, that's why – It's something he doesn't want to think about but it's still a part of his life."

Thence to the show and the scenes described at the beginning of this feature. Back-stage, after the show, Angie was in jubilant spirit until one sticky moment when a reporter from a local Merseyside paper grabs a two minute talk and pushes on one question a little too heavily....

'Would you say you're playing on his name?'

'I don't know', *replied Angie,* 'Am I playing on his name?'

'Well, are you?'

'No, don't ask me. You fucking know.'

The reporter murmurs something incoherent, halting Angie's comment.

'Let me speak. If you're going to ask me questions, let me answer them. David took the name and I helped make the name famous, so if I'm playing on his name, there's your answer.'

The reporter, flustered but undefeated, pursued the line of approach:

'Would you say you're using the name which isn't your surname, on purpose?'

'Well, neither is Jones my surname but that's my legal name and I can't get away from it.'

Eventually, the atmosphere clears and all is well with Angela Bowie and the local reporter. The question is one which Angie must have heard a thousand times since her return to live work – it wasn't the question but the forceful way in which it was asked that she retaliated to. We resume our talk...

What goes through your mind on-stage?

"To make sure it's a good show. It always feels great on stage. I don't feel that the years I spent away from the public eye were wasted because I was always doing things, working in the theatre teaching improvisation. I really enjoy helping other people's performance. The important thing is to give a good show, otherwise you shouldn't be up there. I direct people but I always feel embarrassed in doing so. I was very happy that people seemed to enjoy it tonight. For a first hearing it was very favourable reaction. I never have a problem with audiences because I like them. A lot of performing artists don't like audiences but I do. I work real hard to make them happy. A lot of times you lay yourself open, I hope the audience enjoys what I do. When I do poems I hope they'll enjoy them. If they don't, well, that's a shame, it was my mistake. They weren't in the condition to dig it or I didn't do it well enough for them to enjoy it. But that's the challenge, isn't it? I have a tremendous faith in people. When I used to answer letters for the fan club, I was always totally open and honest, and people could either love me or hate me. When I started performing, an old friend of mine **Leee Black Childers** said 'What if the audience throw things at you?' – That never even occurred to me! How could anyone throw things at me? I love them. They wouldn't do that and if they did, I'd duck because the person would be so stoned or so drunk that they didn't mean to. And if it got too much, I'd go into the audience and punch him in the mouth and tell him to sit down and behave. I don't live in that fear.

David used to fear the audiences in the early days. Gillingham and Gravesend, double gigs, 11.00 and 1.00 in the morning. We did the 11.00 show and by the time of the next show the crowd were drunk and rowdy and you can bet they didn't want to hear 'Space Oddity'. They didn't want to hear a solo folk singer, they wanted **Buddy Holly.** I said to David 'Forget about 'Space Oddity', my friend, we's gonna be dead if you do that.' So I rounded up the support band, asked if they knew any Buddy Holly and said 'Get out there and do 'em!'. So, David went out and did a whole show with the band of Buddy Holly numbers. He got to the end, and did 'Space Oddity'! They start throwing beer bottles. I wasn't too worried about those because I thought any fool could see a bottle coming and be able to duck in time. But then this guy

started throwing lighted cigarettes, he was just lighting them one after the other and throwing them at David. David's got one duff eye and I knew he couldn't see cigarettes coming so I was scared they'd get him. I grabbed the guy and started punching him, then the police came in and arrested me! It took David four hours to get me out of jail! The officer saw me punch the guy 'I saw you do that' – I just thought it would be best not to say anything and go quietly (laughs)."

(Talking of rowdy crowds, one appeared at the dressing room door. The noise level rose considerably and one drunken sot had apparently caught and killed a rat (the size of a cat) holding it aloft by the tail and intending it as an offering to Angie **(he was not a fan).**

'Does anybody realise that a dead rat, like any corpse, is unhygienic?' *said Angie.*

'You should have seen the guy carrying the rat', *said Roger, Angie's friend. The situation, quickly resolved, gave way to humour and the course was clear to continue the conversation)...*

Can we go back to the time you lived with David at his Mother's house? Was his Mother supportive of his career?

"No. It wasn't that she didn't want to be, it's just that she didn't know how. Her husband had done it all. David's dad was so supportive that she really didn't know what to do about it. She did her best."

Why did David decide not to invite her to your wedding?

"I never really knew. She turned up on the day and I was delighted. I thought David had a really silly attitude about his family. He thought he could get rid of them when he didn't want them. And I kept explaining to him you can't get rid of family. Unfortunately, you can't choose them, you inherit them and you just have to be cool."

Did she give you a hard time?

"Not really... It was hard at the time because I had such a good relationship with my parents that I couldn't understand all that snippiness. Then I talked to my mum about it and she said, 'Well, come on, she's just lost her husband, what's the matter with you?' It took my mother to sort me out on it. David's mum went to my parents in Cyprus for six months and that straightened her out. She got to flirt with my dad, and all that good stuff and she was cool. I always took care of her so I think even in her wildest moments she knew I wasn't her enemy.

I had a problem for two or three months

♦ *At the age of 14, Joey Bowie prefers maths and 'Dungeons and Dragons' — At just two years older (16) this is what his father was doing — Pictured with his first group The Kon-Rads performing at a youth club, Lebanon Gdns., Biggin Hill in May 1963.*

Syndication International

I never even knew what the Ivor Novello Awards were, it took me four years to find out they were song-writers' awards and then, the idea of David being honoured as an artist, I probably got madder! Don't get me wrong, it wasn't just me. Ken wouldn't even let David's mum go along. So, I probably said that he was a pig in lieu of the awards. He wasn't that bad really. Just a soppy man."

What about Tony deFries?

"Tony was great. He was a thief and a gangster but if you want to get something done who do you hire? A wal? I actually hired Tony. The only problem was that I was the only one that could control him so when I wasn't around no-one could handle him." *'Didn't David hate him?' came a question from someone else in the room,*"Let me put it this way,"*continued Angie,*"Who do you like when you're really drunk, and I'm being polite, I don't mean drunk."

Keeping the conversation on other individuals who used to be close companions to the Bowie nuclear family, I asked what had happened to Freddi Burretti:

"Freddi is married, living in Haifa and designing knitwear."

Who was actually lead vocalist on the Arnold Corns singles?

"David. We were contracted to Mercury so we couldn't record for them because we were in the process of disassociating ourselves from that label. We weren't signed to anyone else so we couldn't start doing stuff for Bell which is where we released those singles. David was the lead vocalist on that project, it was really him in disguise."

What happened during the period when David decided he couldn't write any more?

because I had never been hated for doing nothing before. You know, I hadn't even done anything. But I was never rude and that paid off. She realised that I wasn't all the things she had imagined."

You once called Kenneth Pitt 'a pig' (as recorded in his book). Was there any reason for this?

"Now why was Ken Pitt a pig? He must have done something in particular which of course I can't now remember. I don't think I'd go that far. He wasn't that bad. Oh! Maybe I

do know why I called him a pig – David got the Ivor Novello Award and wanted to take me to the Awards ceremony and Ken wouldn't have it, under no circumstances. Ken wanted to go on his own with him, which he did. I was pregnant with Zowie and I hated being left on my own. I was real lonely. So if anyone had asked me what I thought of Ken Pitt I probably would have said he was a pig. I thought it was daft, because I never made a fuss over David in public as I knew that Ken wanted to make out he was his piece of trade.

Gina Coyle

♦ *Singing on — Angie Bowie, Liverpool, Feb. 1985.*

♦ *Signing on — David Bowie, New York Jan. 1983 — Note the bracelets.*

"I don't really know. When David had the nervous breakdown he didn't come to me. He went to Coco because Coco's mother was a psychiatrist. David was always a real artist, but the problem was that David was a Yorkshireman, so underneath it all, 'As long as brass is in bank, it be totally cool' so as long as the money was coming in it was fine. When he was spending too much money on drugs, it wasn't cool because he knew he was doing something wrong. He was hooked for two or three years – It was mostly coke. The problem with that drug is that if you have a grasshopper mind it forces you to focus, so anything that helps you to focus you tend to marry. You're in a state of super anxiety, when you do too much you can't sleep, or focus. You're now on a wire, that's when it becomes speed. People say to me 'Oh, why did your marriage break up' and I'd say 'Well, excuse me, but this was not the man I knew. I didn't know him at all'."

Today, the ultra-modern, ultra-wise Angela Bowie seems a happy woman, pushing harder than ever for an individual career. Calmly understanding and not in the least resentful of her ex-husband's distance and general silence, the indications of lasting love and respect are clear. 'I think we watch over each other' says it all... ●

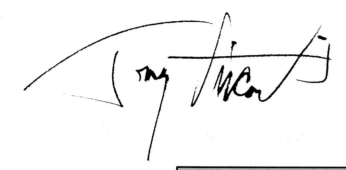

Tony Visconti – A Producer's Tale(s)

Nestling discreetly in London, a stone's throw from Soho's flash-lite centre, Good Earth Studio sits. This is the business home of Tony Visconti, a name commonly linked with some of the world's most acclaimed recording stars.

His involvement with Bowie is far reaching and apart from one or two notable exceptions, he claims the rare honour of holding the longevity record of working associations with a person he himself can only describe as 'incredible'.

From early 60's production work through to the ground-breaking album 'Scary Monsters & Super Creeps' in 1980, Visconti stood always at Bowie's side in the recording studio, helping to define the indefinable and produce coherent realisations of Bowie's ever developing concepts.

With Visconti, David Bowie trail blazed his innovative career through the turbulence of the 70's amassing a mighty back catalogue of musical wizardry.

Tony Visconti is confident, proud of his achievements with Bowie and many other artists, and a very charming American.

Normally reluctant to talk in depth about David Bowie, the following interview sees Visconti at his most candid as he discusses his early memories of life in the Bowie household, the environment in which he and Bowie grew and matured, work in the studio and a subject which is still open to much debate – the working and personal relationship between Bowie and the late Marc Bolan.

The conversation took place at his Good Earth office which is a seductive gallery of sparkling gold records and framed photographs, taken by himself, of the many stars he has produced. (One casual shot of Bowie depicted the not-so serious one grinning broadly, dressed in blue jeans and a white t-shirt with 'I love Switzerland' emblazoned across it.)

Throughout it all, Visconti was informative and pleasant, speaking in a voice with soft traces of a Brooklyn accent diffused over the years with a certain Englishness....

♦ *'All our own work' .... David Bowie pictured with Tony Visconti.*

20

You were born in Brooklyn, New York – Did you have a musical childhood?

"Yes I did – First of all, I was singing ever since I can remember. Both my Mother and Father were natural singers, although not professionally. My father bought me a ukulele for Christmas when I was four years old. It was a Popeye ukulele and it had different coloured strings and a book – So I taught myself to read ukulele diagrams and I knew a lot of chord changes by the time I was five."

Did you have any classical teaching?

"Well, not at that age, but when I was a little older I studied classical guitar from 11 to 14 and then I went to a high school similar to the kind you see in 'Fame'. It didn't have the dance and all that but the music programme was excellent and I was majoring in five music periods each day, giving up my lunch break and physical training. I had quite an extensive musical education there."

How did you first come to England?

"In 1967 I met **Denny Cordell** who was then the producer of **Joe Cocker, Procul Harum, Georgie Fame** and **The Move,** and he had a session in New York. I worked for a publishing company called The Richmond Organisation and was the house producer there, having just got the job and Denny worked for the associate British organisation – Essex Music.

So when we met he was saying 'Oh, we're transatlantic brothers' and I helped him do a recording session for Georgie Fame in New York.

He wanted to do the session British style without any arrangements – just pieces of paper and let the musicians get on with it.

Well, there are union rules against that kind of thing. It's very unprofessional to do that in New York, it's almost professional here if you've got a lot of money, but in New York three hours of musicians' time costs a lot of money as you're always expected to prepare for sessions. So I did a great saving the day act – I wrote out a quick arrangement, xeroxed it and brought it to the studio helping to communicate Denny's intentions to the musicians as well as I could. Denny was an extremely well-spoken Englishman and I could hardly understand him myself coming from New York. So I acted as a kind of translator and it all worked out very well. To cut a long story short, the incident was instrumental in convincing Denny that I was the person he needed to assist him and I came over to England as an assistant producer. That was in 1967 and it was the very first time I'd ever seen England."

Did you like it here at first?

"I loved it. It was everything I'd expected it to be. I saw all The Beatles films over and over. London was everything. Plus, of course, I had this romantic notion in my head which made it what I wanted it to be. London, at that time, was the centre of just about everything – music, fashion etc."

Can you remember the first time you were able to work in a studio?

"Oh yes. I started doing recording sessions in America when I was 13. I was always in neighbourhood groups; always forming bands and I just went in at the age of 13 to do some demos. At the time, I had a best friend who lived around the corner from me who worked for Atlantic Records in their studio. He used to sneak me in on sessions by people like **Aretha Franklin** – just as an observer.

And also, late at night, we'd go in and my friend would explain everything to me. He was very instrumental in giving me my early studio education. I started professional work when I was 16."

Perhaps some people don't realise how important a producer is to a record – Can you explain exactly what a producer does?

"A producer is responsible for the entire production of a record and that begins outside the studio when the producer and artist meet to discuss what material will be recorded and in which way. Also, what musicians to book, if it isn't already a band, what studio and so on. All these things the producer must have a sure knowledge of, because to book the wrong studio or hire the wrong musicians for an artist might be a disaster. He must accept the responsibility of a musical director. When you have an engineer producer, he can do this but mainly checks on the sound, tells someone when they're out of tune etc.

The kind of producer I am is that I can actually step into any job in the studio."

Is it almost like a public relations job as well? Keeping the peace....

"Well, there is that too, but this is a specific relation between the artist and the producer."

When did you first meet David Bowie?

"I was wondering when we were going to come around to this one! (laughs). OK, I'm a bit cloudy about this, but I'm sure that it was at the end of 1967 in the offices of Essex Music where I was employed.

Sean Mayes

Brian Ward

My other boss, **David Platz,** just said: 'We've got this young man and we don't quite know what to do with him. He writes every song in a different style'. I was already involved with **Marc Bolan** at the time and David Platz continued to say: 'Since you seem to be the expert with these strange people – I'd like to see what you can do with this David Bowie'.

So I met him there in the Essex music room. 68 Oxford Street – I know how people like these little details!"

Initial impressions...?

"My initial impression was that he was a nice, well-mannered Englishman. He wasn't the bizarre person that he was made out to be, or would later become. He seemed to want to like me instantly. He liked the fact that I was an American and within 15 minutes we were sharing stories and experiences. We became very close in a very short space of time. I must say that my first impression was: 'I like this person very much'."

It seems that in the early days, great pains were taken by people like yourself and Ken Pitt to keep David's affairs and recording sessions in order. When did you first decide that such effort and tolerance on your part would be worthwhile?

"I believed in David. I wouldn't do anything for anyone unless I thought it would be worthwhile. I loved his songs but I was trying to get him to concentrate on one style of writing as I felt that it was his undoing that he was writing in so many different styles. I remember that when he threw 'Space Oddity' at me, I hated it. I felt 'Who the hell are you'?

You know, he'd just written a string of **Simon & Garfunkel** type songs, 'Janine' and so on – really low-key folksy stuff. And then this. I still don't like 'Space Oddity' all that much, although when I hear it now I realise that I'm listening to a classic recording.

But it was never one of my favourite songs. I had a lot of reasons at the time, but they're probably not valid now so it doesn't matter. What happened with 'Space Oddity', in fact, was that I told him: 'You'll probably have a hit record with this but how are you going to follow it up? – It's like nothing you've ever written before' and, in truth, it wasn't until three or four years later that he did have another hit record. So my prediction was correct in that sense, that he couldn't really follow it up.

I saw that song as a spectacular cheap-shot. Cashing in on the moon landing."

Is that exactly what it was? There's all these different stories. Some saying the inspiration came from Kubrick's '2001'.

"That's exactly what it was and he'd admit it I'm sure.

You know, it was inspired by everything. There's a guy in Beckenham who claims that David stole the story directly from him. But the thing is, David's just a person who, if you talk to him, you run the risk of his stealing some of your material. It happens to everyone in life.

It depends on whether you want to volunteer it or not, but he'll get it. He's a very perceptive lad.

It doesn't matter where he got it from –**Kubrick's** '2001' or whatever, he wrote it to get a hit record and power. And I guess I was

too idealistic in those days and felt he should be more faithful to his own style. This is where we differed on this point. In those days he would do anything to get a hit record."

You said before that David was a mild-mannered Englishman when you met. Has he changed much?

"Oddly enough, he seems to have gone full circle. My last meeting with him, which was August 1983, showed him to still be very mild-mannered and extremely polite. He's also very cultured, he's a world traveller. That's something I always gave him credit for. He never stays in his hotel room, he's always out wanting to know what's happening.

Nowadays, his favourite place seems to be the Far East. He always returns to Japan."

There weren't many reports of David out on the town on the last tour...

"Well, it's getting harder for him all the time. He realises that."

Has his studio working method become more serious as he's got older?

"The last thing I did with David was 'Scary Monsters'. His method's pretty much the same as we set on 'The Man Who Sold the World' in 1970. It's just that he writes at the very last minute. He doesn't get at all nervous about going into a studio beforehand. He has to actually get into the situation of being in a recording studio before he can do anything. At the beginning of albums, he's pretty laid back, smokes a lot, reads the newspaper and gives **Carlos** *(Alomar)* a few chords perhaps.

And fair enough, he does give Carlos credit when he's very instrumental in writing something. It's only when things start

21

happening – David's a great believer in chemistry. There's no chemistry when he's sitting alone at home, but he has this way of getting very interesting people together and then to interact. This is his method."

Has that always been the case throughout David's career, this channelling of ideas?

"Well, yes, he draws people into him but he's not necessarily the channeller, although, in the end, it does all come through him.

They get quite out of control, recording sessions. David would be the last person to admit that he's totally in control of it all. But we do create a context in which creative people can have a lot of freedom.

Ultimately, we wait until everybody leaves before we start editing stuff down. We record a lot of material, there's a lot of tracks that never make the album – backing and totally complete tracks.

You know, totally finished tracks musically, with guitar solos and such like, and if David doesn't feel inspired enough to write the words at the time, they're usually just left like that.

'Fashion' was originally called 'Jamaica'. He was going to write a little ditty about Jamaica but couldn't think of a single thing to write. It almost got thrown away, until at the very last minute he decided to call it 'Fashion'. He must have been talking to someone!

David often lets friends into the studio when he's working. **Iggy** will come along and friends like **Fripp** will walk in. Not to work on the music but just to interact on a conversational level.

You see, when you're getting a David Bowie vocal you're getting very much how he actually felt maybe an hour beforehand."

Does he find it easier to work with other people in the studio, because he's performing to people rather than just a microphone?

"No, they'll go away. He'll send them out and perform just to me because he's not that much of an extrovert, believe it or not! But he'll talk to them, open a newspaper and suddenly say: 'I've got it!' and he disappears for 15 minutes and then reappears in front of a microphone and says: 'OK – Record these two lines'. So he'll sing something like 'Joe the Lion', that's one example of a song that was written this way, just the first two lines then 'Stop the machine'. He'll think for a moment then say 'Drop me in after those

lines'. And slowly, not only the vocal will emerge from this session but the lyric and the melody. On 'Scary Monsters' for instance, only 'It's No Game' and that song by **Tom Verlaine** 'Kingdom Come' were completely finished songs in which we already knew the lyrics, melody and so on."

He seems to like that method of song-writing as he's always enthusing about how good Iggy is at it...

"Yes, that is something he learnt from Iggy, quite honestly."

Can you describe a basic day in the studio with David Bowie? I know you've already gone a long way to doing that but is there any kind of routine?

"One thing where we differ from most people is that we're out of that syndrome of where you get in at 4.00 in the afternoon and leave at 10.00 the next morning. We stopped doing that during 'Young Americans' when we were both silly young men just keeping those hours for the sake of being there. Pushing and pushing ourselves, not really knowing what we wanted. Nowadays, it's a lot clearer of what we both expect from a recording session. A typical session might start at 2.00 in the afternoon – David and the musicians coming in and messing around for a while.

Things happen very quickly, especially around Carlos. And within two hours we'll have something really nice on tape. One reason it doesn't take so long now is that, for example, at the time of 'Low' David was so unsure of this new direction that he said: 'Let's treat the first two weeks as demos'. And after the two weeks had gone I said 'We have much more than demos here, why do we have to re-record all this lovely stuff? So we listened back and the lesson learnt from that is that we keep the machines running while we're creating and we do all the demos on 24-track – just in case. That's been the approach to every album we've done together now and there's no need to go back and re-record anything.

So about 8.00 in the evening David would say 'That's enough' and tell the musicians to go home but he would stay just to do some la-la's or some humming – just to get some ideas down on tape. After that, we'll go out and reward ourselves. Have some dinner, go to a club or see a show and not return to the studio until 2.00 the next day.

So, our sessions last no longer than eight hours and quite often they're as short as six

hours.

Once the backing tracks are finished we send them away. That's like phase one and we never return to it. The next phase is over-dubs and then we bring in people like **Eno** and **Fripp** who are specialists in that field and that's still quite a short day. We bring in people who have hot ideas anyway, who'll do anything. And as it's David they'll usually end up doing anything!

Phase three would be when David does vocals, which is very, very private. Because he's composing on the spot we usually have no unnecessary people present – not even Coco. *(Corinne Schwab – Bowie's personal assistant for many years).* It's just me, an assistant engineer as I'll engineer his vocals and that's it, just three people. Again, these sessions will last only about five hours, after which, we'll go out."

Can you recall any particular humorous occurrences whilst working in the studio?

"I remember when we were doing the backing vocals to 'Red Sails'... The context we set was a Chinese backing track with German backing singers and we all acted the part. There was David, Brian Eno and myself all clenching our fists and singing 'RED SA-AA-AILS!' in very butch voices – really getting into it. All three of us had our eyes tightly closed. Now the studio – Mountain Studios in Montreux is right off a casino and the side door to the studio was left unlocked on this day. Through these doors, in walked these three Swiss waiters dressed in black suits with aprons down to their ankles carrying food for somewhere – obviously they had walked through the wrong door.

I don't know how long they were standing there but I opened my eyes first and said 'Oh my God!' and there I was shaking David to try to get them to stop but the headphones were so loud they were totally into it.

When they finally realised, we all burst out laughing at these waiters standing there with trays of food, jaws down to their knees hardly believing what they were seeing. Of course, I must tell you, it's disembodied singing. To us we had the music in our ears but what the waiters saw were these three maniacs acting like German operatic singers!! You can imagine the cultural clash and what an encounter that was..."

Everyone will think of that now when they hear 'Red Sails'...

"Yes, I'm sure they will (laughs).

Greg Gorman

The next topic of conversation was Haddon Hall, a Victorian red-brick building that housed David Bowie, his wife Angie and son Zowie as well as many other friends and guests in the early 70's. It was here that Bowie's creativity began to develop, eventually to project and formulate the characterisation of Ziggy Stardust. Tony Visconti also had a room there at the time...

Was Haddon Hall a successful commune? I understand it got quite cramped at one point...

"It was successful to the purpose that we were all incredibly poor and originally David, Angela, myself and my girlfriend Liz were going to share it. It was certainly cheap at £8 a week for these massive four rooms and massive hall-way. It's just beautiful – Or was beautiful, it's gone now. *(Haddon Hall was demolished in 1981).*

It was only when we decided that David couldn't go on as a solo artist that we had to construct a band around him – which was Hype or Harry the Butcher or one of the many names he used to have, that we thought we had to get all these people. I'm sure you know

who the original members of Hype were – **Mick Ronson, John Cambridge** and myself. **Woody Woodmansey** eventually replaced John on drums. Also, we had Roger, I never knew his last name as we called him Roger the Lodger – he was our Australian roadie. And so, all these people were sleeping upstairs in the gallery. It all got incredibly funky after a while and I was quite happy in my room.

But as a commune, I'd say no it wasn't successful because if we did have any rows it was about the household money. We always felt it was being misappropriated."

Was anyone appointed some kind of house leader?

"Well, Angela was. And with David, we'd give them all the household money and I remember one day they came back with a Chinese takeaway – for themselves and a couple of tins of beans! I said 'God, you know £8 doesn't go very far these days' and so we immediately accused them of using the household money on their takeaway. Which, of course, they didn't – It's just we were all so terribly poor. We were hungry. But there was

a lot of animosity. Like, Angie assumed the role when she saw us move in. The first thing she did was to go out and get a job as a secretary and it was made clear that my girlfriend had to cook for everyone, which, naturally, she hated.

So it was totally unsuccessful as a commune, I must tell you that. Nothing but animosity flying about everywhere. And, quite honestly, when they started being very open about their sex lives, that's when it got really heavy. They would bring people home late at night and I didn't mind what they did in their bedroom – but these people were trying to get into our bedroom as well!! (laughs)"

You built some kind of studio...

"Yes, in the basement we built a small rehearsal studio. We sound-proofed it and it didn't work. Everyone in Haddon Hall wanted to strangle us! In those days, you know how loud we were, almost a heavy metal band and with Mick Ronson, who's totally deaf in one ear, we had to turn it up loud. Eventually, though, we had to rehearse at low volume.

Haddon Hall was constructive in the way

Mick Rock

that we were able to live and work together. I'm just saying on a day to day basis, on a living basis it wasn't successful. Professionally, it was OK...

Was that the original intention – to establish a creative workshop?

"Well, for David and I. We were going to keep those people out. But when they started living with us it went beyond the original idea."

The Spiders slept on the gallery – Did it lead anywhere?

"No, it went around in a circle. You walked up the stairs and there was a stained glass window at the top then two small staircases on either side of the main steps which lead to the gallery where you could have hung old paintings of dead ancestors, but it went around in a circle and met itself. There were no doors leading off, there might have been, years before, but they were all sealed."

In a few other places where he's lived, David's painted some murals on the walls or cupboards. Did he do anything like that at Haddon Hall?

"No, we didn't own it. We weren't allowed."

Does David do much painting?

"Yes, he does a lot of painting. He never did any at Haddon Hall but when we were doing 'Low' and 'Heroes' he was painting all the time and considering having an exhibition. I think he would have done marvellously well – but I think he's chickened out of that. He was going to do it under an assumed name, which is the stupidest thing in the world when you think about it. I mean, if you're David Bowie and you paint, then you should just put them out and say 'David Bowie's paintings'."

He did contribute some pieces to an exhibition which included the New Expressionist movement in Germany between March 23-25 1983. Mostly lino cuts. And selected paintings have been published in Bowie's 1978 world tour programme. It's been said that a vast collection of art-work has been amassed over the years, most of which will probably never be seen. How would Visconti rate David Bowie's ability as a painter...

"They're very good paintings. A lot of depth and perception in them."

Returning for a brief moment to Haddon Hall – Is it true that David used to collect old cars?

"Well, we had an old Riley which he loved. He only had about three, that was after I left. I mean, looking back on it all now – he really wanted the flat all to himself (laughs). As

soon as we all moved out he brought in loads of antiques, but it was a passing hobby. Anyone who knows anything about David will know that these hobbies last for about a month.

So if you're not there for a month, you might miss an entire aspect of his life! It's come and gone."

Can you tell me about the session for BBC's 'Top Gear' radio programme?

"Oh, I remember it well (laughs)."

It was billed: 'David Bowie & the Tony Visconti Orchestra....'

"That's mainly what it was. Do you know

♦ *Lino cut by David Bowie.*

the titles? Hold on, I have the tape here...

(At this point, we surfaced from the cloudy state of interview conversation as Visconti rose from his seat and proceeded to hunt for the 'Top Gear' tape amongst a library of recordings. Very quickly he located the tape and handed it to me. The box was clean and well-preserved, encasing the original reel to reel recording of the show. The date scrawled on it was May 26th, 1968 and I dutifully made a note of the songs performed: 1. In the Heat of the Morning. 2. Silly Boy Blue. 3. London Bye Ta Ta. 4. Karma Man. 5. When I'm Five.

I asked Tony for a concise list of the musicians making up the Tony Visconti Orchestra and he instinctively re-activated the tape recorder, fingers moving with the

authoritative touch of a seasoned producer...

"It was **Herbie Flowers, Barry Morgan** –the boys, in fact, – Herbie on bass, Barry on drums. The guitarist might have been **John McLaughlin** – might have been. I know that he played the 12-string guitar on the studio recording of 'Karma Man' and I think we kept with him. The string players were, you know just guys booked for the session. After they all went home, David, myself and **Steve Peregrine-Took,** who was also there, did the backing vocals. But it was all done through the BBC. You just told them what you wanted and they would book the musicians for you. They were all guys who would work for £7 an hour. You just phoned up an agency and there they were. Of course, they weren't as well known as they are today."

Your contribution to Marc Bolan's career was also very important. How did they differ? In public, Marc often seemed less intense...

"Marc less intense? Marc was a fucking raging lion! He could be, if he wanted to be, such an obnoxious person. He had such a strong ego and was quite full of himself. Very arrogant, indeed.

Marc in the studio was pure business. For example, when we were making 'The Slider' if he'd booked the studio for three days, he'd make us all stay up for three days and nights and record his entire pieces of the album. For tax purposes he had to record albums out of the country.

David's quite leisurely in the studio, not intense at all when he works. Perhaps people have this image of David with furled brow (laughs) but really, he enjoys his work. He's quite academic. Although it seems that he doesn't have a method, he's always keen to do things differently.

He doesn't run around shouting at people, demanding results. He's quite willing to accept whatever happens. And then he does his little alchemy, his magic to charm people. But he would not order people around, whereas, Marc would say things like 'You fucking get that right' or 'I'm not paying you to eat meals' and stomp around like a little Gestapo. David's really quite liberal."

Maybe where most people go wrong is a tendency to analyse his work too much...

"No, it's good. You can analyse his work. I can tell you that there's a lot of deep thought involved, we'd be mistaken to deny that.

But he does all his introspection at home – All those experiences. There's a photograph

25

behind you of David, myself and **Bruce Springsteen.** It was taken during the recording of 'Young Americans'. After we spoke to him and he left – we did a Bruce Springsteen number! Things like that. It is right to believe that he's a deep person, but a nice person. A NICE person to work with! (laughs).

Were there any plans for David and Marc to write and record together? Ones that almost happened?

"They never actually recorded together apart from 'Prettiest Star'. I know that there's a lot of speculation about this and you can believe what you want to believe, but I was there the whole time and even the albums I was absent on, I can promise you that Marc Bolan never walked in on any session. I got him to play lead guitar for 'Prettiest Star'.

During the 'Young Americans' days David told me that he had recently talked to Marc. I hadn't seen him for a couple of years as we didn't have a very nice break up at the time, although we made it up later. So David stayed up all night with Marc, talking about old times and David was already quite successful in America then which is something Marc wasn't. Marc's way was to slag other people off to make himself look bigger and he tried to have a go at David that night, telling him that he was doing things wrong and David just put him very straight about where he was at, that he wasn't going to break America with his present attitude, that he should bend a little and listen more to American taste.

They did have plans to work together, probably that night. You know, if you'd stayed up all night with me at the end I'm sure we'd say – 'Oh, God – We've solved the problems of the world. Tomorrow we'll get up and do 'em!' It was one of those cases. When they both did get up the next day they didn't feel like doing all the things they had talked about the previous night. But they were always talking. Marc was always saying how he'd write a film and David would act in it. David would never act in a film written by Marc Bolan, he just didn't have that kind of respect for him.

Just casual plans to work together, but they never came to fruition – and I know that."

David once taught you to ski...

"Yes." (chuckles)

Was he a patient teacher?

"Excellent teacher. He's great! I stood up in court for him a few years ago in Switzerland when he was going through his divorce with Angie. I just stood up as a witness. And while I was there he said, 'Why don't we have a skiing holiday? You'll be a natural because of your Martial Arts training'. And, as it happened, I was. My girlfriend twisted her ankle within the first hour, but David had me going down the 1,000 metre slopes two days later. For two days that lad took me up to a little hill and made me walk up and down in that cross-legged position, with the toes pointing in and all that. Yes, he's an excellent teacher – very, very patient.

The funny thing was, his son Joey passed us about eight times going down the most dangerous slopes. He's got all sorts of medals for skiing. And he'd say, 'Hi, Daddy. Hi, Tony'

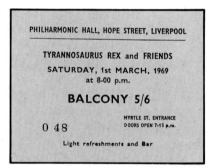

> PHILHARMONIC HALL, HOPE STREET, LIVERPOOL
>
> TYRANNOSAURUS REX and FRIENDS
> SATURDAY, 1st MARCH, 1969
> at 8-00 p.m.
>
> **BALCONY 5/6**
>
> 0 48
>
> MYRTLE ST. ENTRANCE
> DOORS OPEN 7-15 p.m.
>
> Light refreshments and Bar

♦ *Bowie was also on the bill, playing support.*

then zoooom, right past us like a streak of lightning leaving David and I tottering down like old men!

Joey is actually a much better skier than David, but kids are, aren't they? They take to things much easier."

Why does David shield his son so much from the public eye?

"It's a matter of privacy. There's also the danger. Most famous people face the danger of their kids being kidnapped. There are nice people around who would be polite and just wish to say hello, but there's an equal amount of nutters. The man's just being cautious and protective. **John Lennon's** death certainly stopped anyone being very open with the public. I know there's a natural interest amongst David's fans and I can give you some idea of what he's like. He's got blonde hair, very fair and he's a good cross between David and Angela. A very handsome boy, tall, he'll probably grow up to look very much like his father. He's perfectly in line with everything and loves his dad. His dad doesn't always love his taste in music, though (laughs). A couple of years ago, Joey's favourite group were the ELO, which David can't stand. But, you know, father and son are bound to differ on a few points. They absolutely adore each other, I tell you. It's a very healthy relationship. The love in both their eyes when they look at each other is quite astounding."

Going back a few years – Before the arrival of Ziggy Stardust, it's often been said that everyone around David knew that he would soon be very famous. Did he ever show any self-doubt or signs of worry that all these people's expectations might be dashed?

"No. I think once he made up his mind to become famous it was very clear that he had got his purpose in life right. Everyone has doubts, though. You can't function unless you have a certain amount of active nerves around you. I mean, if he did have any great doubts it would never have happened and that's the truth."

I know of your Martial Arts training and also that David once studied Karate –Did you ever practise together?

"No, well, I've shown him some Win Chung and he was very keen, but David lacks the discipline to study anything for any length of time, quite honestly. I'm all for discipline and I've put many years into my training. It's like... David will meet someone, for example – in 1983 he met a nice Chinese girl who taught him some Tai Chi – but only some.

He's very interested in his body and doing something with it but he's far too active to remain in any one discipline for so long. He's very much his own teacher and he uses the world as his school.

He was very proud of the fact that his record producer does Martial Arts. I remember when I first met **Lindsay Kemp,** David said: 'Lindsay, watch this!!' and David made me go through my repertoire for Lindsay who was very impressed and warned me not to do those vigorous exercises in too cold a state – to warm up a little.

Also, on several occasions, David was confident that I was not only his friend but could also act as a bodyguard. There have been some moments when David has been in need of protection. For a person who's so private, he can have these lapses and can go very public all of a sudden. He'll just go out, not tell anyone where he is and end up in some idiotic club at 8.00 in the morning. He usually does this in New York."

I suppose it's good for him to grasp those moments of freedom...

"It's good for him, yes, but it might be dangerous for him as well."

Another of your hobbies is photography. Do you have a vast photographic library of all the artists you've worked with?

"Yes I do and I'm compiling a book of photographs at the moment. They're not artistically great, but they do capture the people I've worked with in natural poses. It's just a matter of sharing, not to make tons of money. I realise now that I have a lot of material and knowledge people would like access to."

It's all very important...

"Yes it is. It's become historical now – Which is why I've come out to talk about it."

Do you have any home movie footage of David?

"No, not David. Marc Bolan yes. I've got loads – about four reels. 'The Tube' only used 11 minutes of it when they put together their special feature on Marc, there's lot's more.

Marc used to like to pose a lot. Whenever I pulled a camera out on David he accused me of being a 'perennial tourist'. Quite often, what would happen in the end was that he'd take my pictures away saying 'Oh, that's great! Can I have a copy of that?' or that it was a good thing that I had a camera to take a picture of it. (laughs)

But really, David's quite camera-shy when he's private and, of course, he never wants a picture of Joey taken. I remember once, I snapped a picture of them together and Joey went right up to his dad and said 'Tony took a picture of me!!!' and looked quite distraught until David said 'It's OK – Uncle Tony is fine'.

I do have a few photos of Joey with my own son Delaney but they're strictly for my own private photo album."

It's interesting that, even so young, Joey has that awareness...

"Well, he was told. You know, when you were young you were told 'Don't accept sweets from strangers'. With Joey, it's 'Don't let anyone photograph you' and, of course, 'Don't accept sweets from strangers either."

Before, you mentioned the original title of 'Fashion' – Can you tell me of any other songs that were originally titled something else?

(At this point, we broke from the conversation as Tony brought out a cassette tape from a nearby cupboard. Recommencing our talk, he quoted from the track listing written on the cassette holder...)

"These are rough mixes – 'David Bowie' 11/3/80 which eventually became 'Scary

♦ *At Haddon Hall*

Monsters'. We have 'I Feel Free' – originally by **Cream**. David used to include that number in the song set sometimes on the 1972 tours. It never worked out though. 'People Are Turning to Gold' became 'Ashes to Ashes'. 'It Happens Everyday' turned into 'Teenage Wildlife'. Instead of singing 'Not another teenage wildlife' he'd sing 'It happens everyda-a-ay'. 'Kingdom Come', 'Up the Hill Backwards' and 'It's No Game' were the same. 'Is There Life After Marriage' was a completely finished track that never actually made the album at all. 'Fuje Moto San' was the instrumental track 'Crystal Japan' – that was its original title. 'Laser' turned out to be 'Scream Like a Baby'. He sung 'I am a laser'. That was a song he originally wrote for the Astronettes in 1973 *(continuity buffs may also be interested to learn that Bowie first recorded 'God Only Knows' by The Beach Boys around the same time)*. 'Jamaica' became 'Fashion' and 'Scary Monsters' and 'Because You're Young' remained the same. So there's a few there."

There's one track which has emerged an audio tape in the Bowie collectors' world over the last few years called 'Tired Of My Life'...

"I've never heard of that one."

It's sung in a very Ziggy '72/'73 vocal style – yet has lyrics from 'It's No Game...

"Really. Well, 'It's No Game' he wrote when he was 16!"

(Upon this revelation, another short break followed. It does seem logical that Bowie would possess a wealth of unused material, but with his constant travelling and changing of habitat, often resulting in much material either being left and forgotten or just disappearing, it is surprising that a song written in 1963 would eventually find a place on an album released in 1980.

When our conversation continued, it seemed the right moment to ask the following question:)

Did you like 'Let's Dance'?

"No. I liked 'Ricochet' and 'Modern Love' very, very much. But not the actual title

Ralph Hulett

track. It was an album he had to make. He told me when I last saw him that he was sorry he didn't use me and that he wanted one of those economical New York type albums. It was very important to him. A new record label, it was what he wanted and he asked if we could work together sometime in the future. I said 'Of course we can'.

We never had a firm contract or whatever to work together. He did 'Station to Station' without me and even two tracks from 'Young Americans' ('Fame' & 'Across the Universe'). It's all right. We have a very healthy relationship.

I was hurt, because I was booked to do 'Let's Dance' and he blew me out two weeks before. This was December 1982 and for four weeks he kept saying 'Keep December free, we're going to go in and record then'.

Getting close to that month, I phoned up Coco and she said: 'Well, you might as well know – He's been in the studio for the past two weeks with someone else. It's working out well and we won't be needing you. He's very sorry'.

I had it out with him in August. It's just that, at the time, I was very hurt that he didn't phone me up himself, which I would have totally accepted. It's just the way he did it that hurt. But I'm off that now (laughs). Sometimes, David has the courage of a lion, but I think that it was just around me that he didn't know how to tell me because we go back ages and all that."

It's often said that David will never tell anyone off or whatever himself. He'll get someone else to do it...

"Yes, well, that's the same for a lot of famous people. They basically don't want to look bad, plus, of course, the opportunity to do that is there."

What was it like working with Paul McCartney?

"All right – Very interesting. The guy's very energetic and knows what he wants. Like all very talented people he obviously has an ego which is something you have to expect. Occasionally, things rub you up the wrong way. So what? It was nice working with him."

This is an obvious question: Do you have a favourite Bowie album of all the ones you've produced.

"I like "Heroes" a lot. There's a lot of me on "Heroes" (laughs). Those three albums – 'Low'/"Heroes"/'Lodger' because it was a wonderful introspective period. On 'Low' both of us were totally depressed. David was going through a divorce and splitting up with a manager and my life was all ups and downs. And we both came out of it by "Heroes". It was just the opposite. We were very optimistic, having a lot of fun. So, I'd say that was my all-time favourite. 'Scary Monsters' I like also, because not only was it a good album but it was also financially successful, which helps, of course. It was the fruition of those three albums. We had created a commercial style which everyone has copied. It really got the synthesiser thing off the ground. We put people like **Gary Numan** on the map."

Has David ever expressed a preference to you?

"He loves 'Low'. It means something to him. He communicated his state of mind very clearly, even though it was a miserable state he did it crystal clear and he was pleased with that. 'Low' presented a very bold musical statement as well. He wasn't playing it safe at all with that album."

A good record to play when you're depressed...

"Yes, music to cut your throat to... (laughs)"

Did you see any shows on the Serious Moonlight tour?

"I saw three shows. I was asked, by David, to attend the show in Edinburgh because his sound was being criticised in the press, and he wanted me to see the show and tell him and the sound engineer what could be improved. My immediate response was 'Why don't you get **Nile Rodgers** to do it?' But I got off my act (more laughs) and flew up to Edinburgh.

So I stomped around in the field in the mud and made a few notes, then I flew back in the private 707 which they had booked for the whole tour. It had a big conference table and instead of seats it has chaise-longues, marble table-tops and a big bedroom in the back. So David, Carlos and myself sat in this bedroom and I confirmed their worst fears about the sound. It was appalling. They said 'OK, will you come to the benefit concert at Hammersmith Odeon and put it right'.

Which I did. I went to the rehearsals and they just literally let me have the board, so I did the sound that afternoon and left it for the engineer. He didn't like what I had done. He was an American Texan who was used to putting out big bass, snare drum and vocals. They don't believe in clarity. Whereas, British records have a lot of clarity on them, American records tend to be very thuddy. So he was trying to produce an American sound

◆ *Tasting the ashes of success?*

with what is basically very British music. Ultimately, we had a bit of a row, but then David jumped from the stage and I asked him what he thought of it. 'Sounds great', he said and 'Will you do the rest of the tour with me?' I said 'No way. I've got a vacation booked with my kids who have only three weeks off this summer. I can't follow you around the rest of the world.' 'At least do Madison Square Garden with me' he said, but the answer was basically no – I just couldn't drop all my plans for the year.

I haven't heard from him since (laughs). I sent him a birthday card so I hope he's not holding it against me. He shouldn't do because it really wasn't my tour, it was his. They waited until the very last moment to get a sound guy. They should have thought about that."

Were you surprised with the popularity he gained in 1983?

"Oh, no – It was bound to happen. I wasn't surprised at all."

Are there any other artists you'd like to work with?

"Not really. I feel that I've had a wonderful career, a very interesting life and I want to produce people who just want to make great records. I'd like to work with David again, that's for sure. Also, I'd like to write a lot of my own stuff now and produce it – not as a

singer but as a composer."

You released one album of your own...('Inventory' in 1977)

"Yes, that was a disaster. Well, it wasn't a disaster, just an OK album. But now, I'd like to get people to sing my material and also to write some music for films. At my advanced age, which is 40, folks, I think it's the best thing for me to do.

I'm not impressed by a lot of the younger groups coming up now, especially the synthesiser groups. Quite honestly, it's very easy to make music on that level. All the artistry is gone.

It's very much a writer's market at the moment. Everyone I've worked with lately are writers and the first thing they own up to is they can't play and can I do something about it. I've even worked with a lot of young groups who don't even want the responsibility of playing and that's ridiculous.

David's about the only person I'd like to work with again, truth to tell..."

To close then, if someone came up to you and asked you to describe David Bowie in just one word. What would that word be?

"Incredible." (Spoken with a beaming smile)...

Tape ends....... ●

Kenneth Pitt

Kenneth Pitt – Managing a Legend

Kenneth Pitt was born and educated in London. Although he studied at the Slade School of Fine Art at London University, he took up commercial art and advertising as a career. He combined this background with his interest in music which eventually led him into the world of public relations. In 1951 he made his first visit to the States where he signed contracts to handle British publicity for some of the top bands and singing stars of America. A man of undoubted integrity, Pitt remained Europe's leading publicist throughout the entire 50's. Meanwhile, he was becoming aware of his aptitude for management.

As the 60's dawned, Pitt was already established as a highly respected publicist-manager and not the least of his qualities was his youthful outlook and ability to stay abreast of the times. With the 60's beat boom, he managed the country's third most successful group **Manfred Mann.**

In 1964 Pitt helped to launch **Bob Dylan** in Europe, the same year Manfred Mann had a hit with 'Do Wah Diddy Diddy' and toured the world.

In 1966, Pitt financed the making of a record by **Crispian St. Peters** called 'You Were On My Mind' which became a massive world hit.

When Pitt accompanied Crispian St. Peters to New York he brought with him an acetate copy of a new single to play to **Walt Maguire** of London Records. It was called 'Rubber Band' and was by a young writer/singer whom Pitt had been nurturing. His name was David Bowie, and Maguire remembers Pitt describing the young man as 'someone very special'.

Throughout the furious 60's, Kenneth Pitt handled Bowie's budding career, pushing and guiding and assisting that first difficult step on to the ladder of success....

32

because his father died before I really got to know him."

Did he talk about his half-brother Terry much?

"Yes, Terry was very much David's hero at the time. I remember one particular day David came to see me and was in a very good mood as he told me, 'Terry's just come home from the Merchant Navy' – He was very pleased."

Going back to the days when David was living with you in Manchester Street – Could you give us a typical day in the life....?

"Yes, well, half the day was spent trying to get him out of bed, then trying to get him to eat, then saying 'Oh, not another cigarette, David' and that was the routine at the time. I never really saw him early because I was up and out to the office. At that time my office was in Curzon Street and we were living in Manchester Street, so any communication was via notes left on the kitchen table. But then, the routine was that at about noon when he surfaced, he would telephone the office to say *(takes on desperate vocal style)*, 'Hello, I'm up', and then say, 'What are we doing for lunch'. And then I suppose he would come to the office and would go off to the interviews and whatever else we had arranged. There wasn't that much to do at the flat, really, we were rarely there. He didn't eat much while we were there, in fact, he didn't eat a lot at all. It was quite remarkable how he kept alive. He was all coffee and cigarettes, coffee and cigarettes. Of course, he did cook when he made up his mind to. He would be a great, masterful cook for that week alone. I remember once we went through an Eastern cooking time – it did dreadful things to my digestion! Things would be put in the fridge and forgotten. You would hear something barking in the fridge and it was something he had cooked a month beforehand."

I believe that you have come across some uncatalogued demo discs from way back that you have now catalogued....

"He was very clever with the things he used. He used to create his own synthesizers and he would have books and jam jars and all sorts of things that he would create his own synthetic sounds on. I think the whole 'Space Oddity' demo was created out of all sorts of funny things. He would set up piles of books to get different drum sounds. It was remarkable.... like, six encyclopedias would

KENNETH PITT first saw the young Bowie during one afternoon's performance at the Marquee. At the time, Bowie's stage act was not quite so elaborate as it is today, and Pitt's first glimpse of a talent that would one day shine consisted of mostly solo acoustic numbers performed by an eager 19-year old.

In those days, however, Bowie still attracted a loyal following and as Pitt remembers 'He always had a fan club ever since I knew him. The earliest one was run by two girls that lived in the road where he did.'

Upon mutual agreement that Pitt could help further Bowie's career, Pitt became his manager and heralded the beginnings of an association that would carry the young and impressionable Bowie through the 60's,

eventually arriving at the hit record that had been Bowie's dream for so long....

Was Bowie as elusive to you as to others about his early background?

"You could never question him. David was never that sort of person – he just used to shrug his shoulders. I did meet his parents and got on with them very well. David's mother often used to watch David perform at the Marquee. I can't remember seeing his father at any performances, although I do remember that David was once asked to make a personal appearance at Brands Hatch for some radio broadcast from there and his parents drove him down. I do remember his parents coming to watch some filming for 'Love You Till Tuesday'. It was a shame be a bass sound and another would be another tone and so on. Eventually, when he wanted to record, he would go all over them like a drummer does and reproduce those sounds. And then he would over-dub all the time.

There are several things I have including various tracks that no-one else has heard of, and he's probably forgotten about them as well. He used to do a lot of recording and I suppose every song he ever wrote in those days was put on tape, either at the flat or at Plaistow Grove. His little room at home was at least two inches deep in tape."

How did David feel about his early fans?

"Well, he never really thought he had fans as such. He never had any friends who were fans. He couldn't relate to that type of person. David would often come down to my office and bother the girls there. They would come up to me and say, 'All right if we go and have a coffee with David?'. And then they'd all go off. David used to spend a lot of time in coffee bars – never paid for his coffee, though, always got it free!"

Do you think that if David had stayed with you he would have been able to do all the things he did?

"He would have achieved as much and I am certain he would have done everything better. He would be further ahead than he is now. He wasted five years. He would be five years ahead of his time if he had stayed with me.

I think that he is of a different mind now, and that we both probably have a great deal in common. I think that the problems that are likely to confront him today are those that I think I could answer.

I am impressed by the way David is handling things now, though. It's suddenly all going right for him. He grew up. Well, he's got this background of success and he feels more secure. Now I think he can sit back and rest a bit.

He's got the money now which I am very glad about, he's worked hard enough for it."

Are there any questions about the past you have always wanted to ask David but have never had the opportunity to do so?

"No, there are lots of things I could ask him but it would be unwise to do so. David is a person that tends to shut history out, and I don't think he really likes to talk about his past. The way he says he never keeps any of his own records and the way he denies things from the past, shuts them out. He might become a little irritated."

CAN'T
HELP
THINKING
ABOUT
ME

Ken Pitt

♦ *Little Toy Soldier.*

Do you think he'll ever get another manager?

"He's got managers. He's always had people handling his affairs. He just hasn't got one individual. It's not like it used to be, he doesn't need that particular type of personal management. Someone who helps him to get bookings.... he doesn't need that, not with all the offers and parts pouring in."

When you were his manager, did you worry about the money you were losing?

"No, because I knew that one day I would get it back, that David would make it. I was always out of pocket by thousands. In the long term, though, I haven't lost out."

Do you know if David is ambidexterous?

"What? Oh, I thought it was another one of those carefully disguised bi-sexual questions. (laughs). Actually, I don't know. I do remember that he used to have a curious way of writing. *(Picks up a pen and writes in a very uncomfortable position).*

His handwriting was always quite atrocious though.

He always used to handwrite his songs at first, then type them up on an old typewriter he had in his room. I still have a lot of his typewritten material and if it gets mixed up with my stuff I can always tell his style. His typing was totally different to anyone else's – always different!"

What did Christmas mean to him – Did he go home?

"Christmas meant a lot to him. He used to worry a lot about how we would be able to afford to buy presents, and we would put our heads together and discuss ways that he could earn £20 or whatever to buy them."

Ken suddenly goes to the bookshelf and brings back a book of children's poems illustrated by Caldecott. The inside cover read in typical Bowie handwriting 'To Ken, very best wishes for '68, Bowie.'

"Yes, he would enjoy Christmas. He did go home."

Did you draw David's interest towards films?

"When I met David, he was obviously interested, had ideas in his head, but the conversations we had drew those ideas out and made them credible. Before he met me, he'd never been to the theatre at all so I introduced him to that. Theatre was always a big part of my life.

When David walked out on stage for the first time as the 'Elephant Man', he was working on skills he developed when he was working with me and all those other things he was involved in. Everything mattered."

When he left Manchester Street, did he leave much behind?

"Yes, he did and I still find things knocking around today. Actually, a funny thing happened on the way to the interview. I went to blow my nose and discovered this – *(Pulls out a 'D' monogrammed handkerchief)*. I suppose everything is a treasure. He would come in, this is where he was interesting, he would come in with these odd things that he picked up in shops, and one time he had got some dried leaves and had put them into a little pot. They're still the same today and I've still got them in my study. He also had lots of different Buddhist things, pictures and prints and bookmarks. Lots of art objects. He used to buy them at some kind of antique supermarket owned by some friends of his. I think that they used to let him have stuff a lot cheaper than usual. He managed to get hold of some quite nice items. Later, when he started to get bigger cheques he would start bringing in glassware, Lalique and that sort of thing."

When you were researching your book (The Pitt Report) did you try to find people like Ralph Horton?

"Yes, well I couldn't find Ralph at all and I'm very sorry about that because I've written about him a great deal in the book but I'm very conscious of the fact that it's all my viewpoint and, to a certain extent, David's viewpoint as well. I am critical of Ralph in the book and I don't think you can criticise someone unless that person is there to answer back. I would have loved to have sat down with Ralph and gone through the whole thing. Ralph had a whole scene going with David long before I came along and he could have told me a lot. I alway respected him for getting out of David's life as quickly as he did. He had worked very hard for David and was dedicated to him. But he was out of his depth and that's why he came to me. I was a professional manager, whereas he had been just a roadie, trying to get work and at the same time was trying to keep The Lower Third and The Buzz together. It's just that he wasn't a businessman and let opportunities for David slip by, and the great problem was that he just couldn't handle money. When it did come along he blew it very quickly. David was alway broke, his affairs were in a dreadful mess and it was getting very, very

worrying. Well, when I say he was looking after David's finances, there wasn't much to look after really, he was always on the breadline. But in cases like David's then, you had to do a Margaret Thatcher and handle the economy! Ralph, I'm afraid, if he was given £35 would spend £36. But he bowed out very graciously. David just went to see him one day and had a conversation then he bowed out from then. We heard from him for a few months after that, he was always very friendly and then he disappeared completely."

You don't much like Bowie's film roles do you...?

"Not really. Especially the first two – 'The Man Who Fell to Earth' I disliked for a number of reasons. I thought that David was manipulated by that director (**Nicolas Roeg**) for his own devices. I mean, that director has got a thing about rock stars. David should really have known better and, in fact, he nearly got out of it, had second thoughts, but it was too late. 'Just a Gigolo' was simply a dreadful film. If I had still been David's manager, he would never have appeared in that film."

The complete story of David Bowie's constructive period spent under the management of Kenneth Pitt was told in Pitt's own diary of the time 'The Pitt Report'. He told me that Bowie wasn't the biggest thing to happen in his career and having taken the time to look a bit closer, I can believe it.

Do you think you have been lucky in your career?

"Oh yes, definitely. To do anything comparable today would be impossible. What are the chances today of going into a café and finding another David Bowie? No, today the music business is completely different altogether..." ●

Sean Mayes – Fumble Pass Hero

A David Bowie tour is something which most admirers consider to be the most eagerly anticipated event in the Bowie calendar of all.

In 1978, Bowie embarked on his most extensive jaunt around the world thus far, which took him and his band to areas he had not previously played. Promoting a characterless show with a good degree of regained confidence in himself and his work, Bowie's '78 "Heroes" tour received almost universal praise wherever it played.

On all previous tours Bowie had consistently shown an uneasiness with his audience, hiding true emotion behind an endless succession of stage personas and seemingly going to every length to ensure the safe concealment of David Jones – cocooned snugly from all prying eyes.

The 1978 world tour saw an end to all that.

Sean Mayes joined the touring band to play piano for the 'new' David Bowie after providing piano backing for Bowie's second and (so far) last appearance on 'Top of the Pops' performing "Heroes" in September 1977.

Four years earlier, as a member of the group **Fumble,** he had known Bowie as the carrot-topped space face Ziggy Stardust after supporting the British and American tours of 1973.

Sean, possessed of a pixie-like youthfulness, complete understanding of the fun aspect of rock and roll, and still fully active in the music business with the group **Boysie,** became a close companion to David Bowie as he and the '78 touring party wound their way across countless cities all over the world, sharing the highs, the lows and the euphoria of a mighty musical runaway train.

38

"I WAS born in March, 1946. I went to various different schools as we used to move around a lot, but this was mostly in the South West of England. I started to play piano at the age of 7, but this was just for fun. It was never taken seriously, although my teaching was classical and, I think, classical music is still my first love. Then at 18 I heard 'Twist and Shout' and then I discovered the excitement of rock 'n roll.

On to Cambridge University where I studied philosophy and I was in a couple of soul bands there. This was in the height of the 60's, so it was a lot of fun being near to London. We would often come down to see **Jimi Hendrix** and **The Who** – close enough to reach out and touch them if you wanted to. I never saw David play at the Marquee at the time. The first time I ever saw him was when Fumble joined him on tour in '72. I was very much aware of him, though. I had some of his early single releases on tape and remember thinking at the time that he was someone who sounded very interesting."

Fumble was being termed as a rock 'n roll revivalist group....

"We started out in 1967 as a beat group. This was just after I'd left Cambridge. We were originally called 'Baloons' and we toured Europe. Then we decided to do 50's sound material as it was the best thing we could do out of all the various material we played. We became a very popular live band, playing at every college up and down the country. We supported **Bill Haley** and **Fats Domino** as well.

In 1973 we played the Reading Festival and were among the three most popular acts along with **Rod Stewart** and the **Alex Harvey Band.**

Fumble has continued right up to today, with varying degrees of success. I think that we always had much more success as a live band and accepted that was the way it would be. Technically, we're not together now as Fumble but occasionally we might get together to play the odd gig here and there.

Our involvement with Bowie started in December 1972 when he first saw us playing the Old Grey Whistle Test and probably thought it would be fun to have a 50's band supporting the futuristic Ziggy Stardust.

We did the British and American tours of 1973. For the UK he already had a support in **Stealers Wheel** who weren't a very good warm-up band.

Bowie needed a band who could warm an audience up in half an hour which Fumble were guaranteed to do. We missed the London gigs and started up North. That was all tremendously successful."

Do you remember your first meeting with Bowie?

"He was around, but during that UK tour we were very much on the other side of the security which was very strong then, partly because it wasn't really necessary, but this was part of the big Bowie build-up.

They wouldn't allow us back-stage at all. We had to have a dressing room in a separate part of the building. In Glasgow, we'd just performed an encore and had to leave through this stage door which connects to an alley running along the side of the Apollo. This was a big Bowie show and there were just two girls waiting outside. We were laden down with guitars and the girls rushed us screaming, only to be held back by these two policemen (laughs). At the time, we wished the press could have had a picture of these two lone girls being held at bay at this big Bowie show. We were just fed up of having to sneak around buildings."

(Such tales of unneeded security around the rise of Ziggy Stardust are many. One such concerned the incredible publicity stunt of Bowie's management hiring a concert hall, quickly slapping 'sold out' stickers all across it, and piping taped music out through the sound-systems while Bowie sat around in an empty hall until the show had supposedly ended. Whether such tales are true or not is debatable, although they certainly helped create the mysterious aura that promoted Bowie at the time.)

"At the end of the last gig, I think it was Peterborough, Bowie just came up to us and started talking to me about anything and everything. And then he suddenly said 'Oh, by the way, we'll be going to America soon and I thought it would be nice if you came too'.

So I quickly replied 'Yes, we think that'll be nice as well', or something equally inane like that. (laughs). Then he was called away to a soundcheck and that was that.

The next time we saw him was when we flew out to Philadelphia. Again we missed the first few shows on the tour because our visas didn't come through in time. But on the American tour we became quite friendly with him. Because of the budget we were still staying in cheap hotels while he was in expensive ones, but we saw a lot more of him during that period."

How did Bowie come to choose you and the band for the 1978 tour?

"I was quite curious as I'd heard nothing from him for five years. Then out of the blue came a phone call to do "Heroes" for 'Top of the Pops' and then the tour, so I asked him about it – whether he had checked out my work in the meantime. 'Oh, no', he said, 'I just hoped that you'd be the same as when you were with Fumble', adding 'And you are. Exactly the same' and laughed. I wasn't sure whether he meant that as a compliment or not (laughs).

As for the other members.... He used his basic rhythm section whom he'd worked with for years – **Carlos Alomar, George Murray** and **Dennis Davis** – and four new people: myself on piano, **Adrian Belew,** who'd been playing with **Frank Zappa** when Bowie spotted him and asked him if he'd like to play on the tour, and **Simon House,** the violin player, who was actually at school with David and hadn't heard from him since those days.

Brian Eno wasn't able to tour due to health reasons so David asked him who he would recommend for keyboards. The guy Eno suggested couldn't make it but in turn recommended **Roger Powell** and Roger was taken up from that. What was nice about the '78 tour was that David had chosen us for our individual abilities and didn't really interfere with us much. So the music found its own level and became very much the band's music played in our own way.

We rehearsed for two weeks only. It was extraordinary to get a two hour show together in that amount of time. Carlos was the band-leader and got things into order. He, of course, was very familiar with David's music. David wasn't there for the first few days and when he first arrived he said, 'Let's do the whole of the Ziggy album. That'll surprise 'em!' So we rehearsed the entire album and finally David decided which songs stayed in the set."

Was there any preference from Bowie of an individual show on the tour?

"No, not really. From what I've heard of him talking generally he tends to prefer the early stages of touring rather than the later stages. I think that it's more a matter of what everyone enjoyed. For example, the Melbourne show where it was absolutely pouring with rain. All the audience was drenched with their make-up smeared and everyone on stage was frightened of getting

The announcement, Courtesy Melody Maker

13 concerts, ticket prices, how to book

THE BOWIE TOUR

DETAILS WERE announced this week of David Bowie's eagerly-awaited early summer tour of Britain. He plays a total of 13 major concerts — three each in Newcastle, Stafford and London, and four in Glasgow.

These shows will be the first time he has performed in this country since his "Station To Station" Wembley gigs in 1976, and his first appearances in provincial cities since his "Aladdin Sane" tour in 1973.

The dates are NEWCASTLE City Hall (June 14, 15 and 16); GLASGOW Apollo (19, 20, 21 and 22); STAFFORD Bingley Hall (24, 25 and 26); and LONDON Earls Court Stadium (29, 30 and July 1).

Bowie will be supported by a re-shaped backing band, comprising three old faithfuls and three newcomers. The three who have previously worked with him are guitarist Stacey Heydon (who last played here on Iggy Pop's tour in the autumn), drummer and percussionist Dennis Davis and bassist George Murray.

The new men in the band are Simon House of Hawkwind on electric violin, Fumble keyboards player Shaun Maves and Roger Powell from Rundgren's Utopia on synthesiser.

Prior to coming to Britain, Bowie undertakes an extensive American tour, opening on the West Coast on March 29 and

taking in nearly 60 different locations through April and May. By the time he finishes his final London date on July 1, it's estimated that he will have played to over a million people.

Tickets for Bowie's gigs are obtainable now, and apart from Stafford, are available by post only.

NEWCASTLE: Tickets priced £6, £5 and £4 from City Hall Box-Office, Northumberland Road, Newcastle-upon-Tyne 1. Limited to four per applicant. Make cheques and POs payable to the addressee.

GLASGOW: Tickets priced £6, £5 and £4 from Apollo Centre, 126 Renfield Street, Glasgow. Limited to four per applicant. Cheques and POs to "Apollo Centre Box-Office".

STAFFORD: This venue is unseated and tickets are all at the one price of £4.50, limited to six per applicant. They can be obtained by post from M.A.M. Promotions Box-Office, 24–25 New Bond Street, London W.1., marking the top left-hand corner of the envelope "Bingley". (Cheques and POs to "M.A.M. Promotions Ltd"). They are also available to personal callers at Mike Lloyd Record Shops in Hanley, Newcastle-under-Lyme and Tunstall, and at Lotus Records in Stafford.

LONDON: Tickets priced £5, £4 and £3 from M.A.M. Promotions Box-Office, 24–25 New Bond Street, London W.1., marking the top left-hand corner of the envelope "Earls Court". Limited to six per applicant. Cheques and POs as for Stafford.

an electric shock. But it pulled us all together, the audience and the band, and it created a very enjoyable show.

There were one or two shows that were distinctly not enjoyable, of course. The only real trouble we ever had was in Marseilles, a rough area. The PA blew up during the show. We were performing 'Blackout' funnily enough and that's exactly what happened! Carlos was very quick-witted and shouted for us all to get off stage *très vite!* There was no real division between the audience and the back-stage area and it was felt that we should leave the building. **Keith Richards** once told David that the Stones had chairs thrown at them in Marseilles.

Eventually they managed to prevent a riot and patch up the equipment so we were able to return to the stage. It was like giving a

show to the troops just behind the front line. It was a hell of a show because everyone had so much nervous energy."

How does Bowie react to mistakes on-stage during the actual show?

"Never turns a hair. If he wanted to comment on anything I think he would do so through Carlos. Carlos would be more likely to make any remarks. The only real revision of changes was when we taped the live album 'Stage'. We had to slow the tempos right down for recording."

Was it easy to get to know Bowie throughout the year?

"Oh, yes we became very good friends. We found it easy to get to know each other properly, partly because we were both English and I suppose because I am gay and David certainly *once* was. Also I got on very

Gina Tyler

◗ *Meeting fans in Chicago, 1980, following a performance of 'Elephant Man'.*

well with Coco, so I was often invited out.

I can call him a friend, but one which I seldom see, although I have a lot of friends all over the world that I also see very rarely.

Obviously, there are great areas of him of which I know nothing about. Whenever I saw him he was always very cheerful, and he obviously gets depressed a certain amount but whenever he was depressed he would always keep to himself. So I never saw that side of him. Socially, what would happen when we hit a new town was that Dennis would sort out the jazz clubs and I the gay clubs. I was the only other gay person in the band, but on the whole the clubs were generally more relaxed and played better music. So if David wanted to go out he'd call either Dennis or myself to find out the best places to go."

Was there ever the feeling that you had to be very guarded in what you said to Bowie in case you might inadvertently offend him?

"I think I sensed early on... (pause). It's very silly of him because he's very intelligent and remembers everything he reads. You see, he has such an interest for everything that it all sticks. But he hasn't had a lot of formal education and I suspect he's slightly wary of people that have had a lot of education or are real specialists in their field. It's silly of him, but I think he's frightened of having areas of ignorance shown up.

For example, he might talk about astronomy or black holes and he'd have some really fantastic ideas but maybe one or two facts wrong. It was not the thing to jump in and say, 'Ah, David, that's not quite right', simply because he'd clam up and that would spoil the conversation. That's not just true of David, of course, it's the same for a lot of other people."

(David Bowie's description of a black hole: "When a huge star collapses upon itself the implosion can be so massive that it leaves nothing but an immense gravitational force. If an object should fall into a black hole it would, in theory, reach a point where it travelled faster than the speed of light, which is supposed to be the ultimate speed anything can travel at. So you would overtake your light and your integral being would fall past that threshold going into the hole and possibly, an alternative universe. But your light would remain stuck at the threshold point...." He distorts his mouth and arranges his arms in a ridiculous flailing 'falling' stance and holds, for a second, like a fly in amber, static, pressed against the side of an invisible glass wall. ".... and thus your image would remain on the edge of that black hole forever!" Teeth bare, five second stare).*

Did Bowie ever tape any show for his own private use?

"Every show is taped. The tapes are very carefully guarded by Carlos. Carlos, in fact, would listen to each show through, but I don't know what notes David kept."

It's often been said that he doesn't care much for keeping things for posterity.

"Yes, well, that's characteristic of very creative people. It's what they're doing now that's important and they don't gloat over past things. It's those to whom creativity doesn't come very easily that tend to gloat. David isn't at all like that."

To expand on that – You played piano on 'Lodger' – Does Bowie think how the new material will translate on to thousands of fans?

"When he's finished an album – I saw him in London, in fact, just after he'd completely finished that album, the vocals were all laid down after the tour, and he played me a tape through and asked me what I thought of it. I'm terrible when it comes to hearing music for the first time and passing judgement. I have to listen to it a few times before I can get to know it. I remember with 'Lodger' he was quite down, which is usual for creative people after they've been involved in something for any length of time. It's almost an anti-climax when it's all over. But he was worried about 'Lodger', he didn't think it would be well received. He was worried initially, but at the same time he was saying 'I know that I'm going to feel differently in a few months' time'. Tony Visconti said that he was always like that. Also, when we were doing 'Lodger', he didn't use Roger Powell when the band were all together and I felt along with the rest of the band that he really should have been there. David at the time was concentrating very hard on the album, so it wasn't the right time to say such things.

That was the time when I felt the least close to him. It was a totally different working relationship. He was always happy and often kidding around, but everyone knew that they had to concentrate all the more harder."

Did you like the album yourself?

"Some tracks I love; others I'm not so keen on. I think 'Scary Monsters' was much stronger but that's a general opinion anyway. I was disappointed that he didn't do more tracks from 'Lodger' on the last tour – 'Boys Keep Swinging' especially. I saw Carlos during the Wembley gigs and he explained that in the early stages of the tour David's voice was in pretty bad condition, which is normal after solid rehearsals, and those tracks are particularly demanding. 'Yassassin' would have been another very good live number, but doing a song from almost every album it's understandable why he didn't use too many from 'Lodger'. I felt the 1983 shows were impressive, although a little

*From 'The Thin White Duke Has Gone' by Tim Lott, Record Mirror Sep. 24, 1977.

RCA

Sean Mayes

♦ *Portrait of the artist at work: David in the studio recording 'Lodger'.*

too slick for my taste. It was like... 'You've bought the K-Tel album, here's the K-Tel tour (laughs). The songs were going by so fast there wasn't enough time to clock them."

Would you like to tour with Bowie again?

"Well, let's say I'd enjoy it very much. But it's not a burning ambition. You see, I enjoyed '78 so much it might not be a good thing to go back. I was working with **Tom Robinson** when the '83 band was assembled which was very important to me so I wasn't at all disappointed. In fact, I wouldn't have been able to join if the chance arose.

Live work is my main love. I find studio work interesting but less enjoyable. At the moment, I'm working with the group **Boysie**.

When I was 21, starting out with Fumble, I wanted to be a famous face but having seen that side of it with the Bowie tour, all the pressures involved, I don't think I could cope with it and I realise now I don't wish to be personally famous. Creatively, I'm more likely to bash at a typewriter than a piano, writing prose, not lyrics.

Musically, I just like playing live and I hope I'll be doing that for a very long time...."

There now follows extracts from Sean Mayes' mammoth diary of the 1978 tour, never before published ....

Random extracts from the personal diary of Sean Mayes covering the 1978 tour

Oslo and other shows:- People try to get D's attention for a moment – not, I think, to communicate anything, but to occupy a brief instant of the Divine Consciousness. The time it takes people to recognise a song – some at the first notes, others as the intro gets underway, many not reacting till the vocal starts. And something which amuses me – partly because I think I can understand it – is the way people with cameras suddenly take a photo when they realise he's doing 'Jean Genie' (for example). They want to feel – this is a photo of David actually singing 'Jean Genie'! Though whether they ever identify the pictures afterwards I can't imagine. Groups of people who nudge, hit, grab each other as they notice something special – when he drops to one knee, or kicks one leg out, crosses his hands like a bird's wings. All his movements are extraordinarily graceful and beautiful and none seem without meaning. It is like a continuous choreographed dance – only more spontaneous.

David fielding flowers, balloons etc. and getting much applause.

Guy clambers over the barrier – David goes forward instinctively to grab his collar so he won't fall. Others (our people) go forward to catch him then release him to the local security guys who return him roughly to his seat, D leans over and taps one of them on the shoulder, wags a finger at him – No!

The crowd with one accord rise to their feet....

Amsterdam:- I find it entertaining to observe the different ways people in clubs react to David. Of course, there's the handful of ultra-discos where there's hardly a ripple – everyone is so bored tripping over superstars to pay them any attention. But in the next league down there's a distinct electric shudder and you catch discreet glances, people nudging and whispering. A few smile and say 'Hi David'!

But we had picked somewhere different again. The kids in this Amsterdam night-club were doing double-takes, staring openly then grabbing their friends to tell them the news. We seemed to be in some kind of licensed youth club and I doubt if even a starlet had ever set foot in the place. "I think it may be time to move," I muttered. David hadn't even

noticed, as I think he was hoping to relax and remain incognito by not catching people's eyes. No chance! We were soon in the car heading for the next address.

The streets were narrow, the car nosing its careful way across the small humpback bridges. David fancied walking anyway, so the driver followed in the limousine. Occasionally, we would pass people and sometimes a kid would recognise David and shout something, though they seemed puzzled at the situation of David Bowie walking the streets with a car following. Sometimes a bunch of kids would brush past us without a glance, then peer into the limo to see if anyone famous was inside. Things finally became farcical when Tony decided to ride and started shouting out to passers by, 'Hey, that's David Bowie!'

The club we finally arrived at looked like a disaster to me right from the start. The men on the door looked like the usual monkeys in penguin suits and they wanted to charge us all entrance. Now, there is no reason in principle why we shouldn't pay, we could certainly afford to. But the sort of place which feels it should charge David Bowie is probably full of boring businessmen being fleeced on cheap champagne by bored hostesses — the rip off scene. If they don't think their clientèle are going to be glad to see David, you can bet your sweet ass we ain't going to be panting to see them.

I murmured my feelings to Coco, who agreed, and we made signs to David, but I think he felt he couldn't back out just because someone had asked him to pay, and he was delving deep in his pocket to cover the whole party. I decided, perhaps a little unfairly, that if David couldn't sort this one out, I would leave him to it. So — 'See you in Bonaparte's' and Coco and I ducked out into the street. I was damned if David was paying for me to visit somewhere like that.

A few minutes later we were in Bonaparte's which was filling up nicely and it wasn't long before David joined us there. We soon met some congenial people and talked and danced.

As we were splitting up for our hotels, Coco complained, 'Oh God, I've got to get up early and pack — my room looks like a bomb hit it.' 'Haven't you packed yet?', asked David, surprised. 'No, darling', replied Coco, 'I was packing your things for you!'

Brisbane:- Had a solitary dinner in the hotel restaurant — Pat, Rick, Coco and David appeared back from a Japanese dinner.

David, a little drunk, put his arm around me and asked me what was happening. He decided to come with us to a club I'd had recommended to me if we could find it. We were in the lobby and flicked through the bookstand. I saw a magazine called 'Young Australians' and suggested it as a song title. David saw a book by **Herman Hesse** and decided to pinch it. He held it down by his side as we strolled out, then stuffed it down his baggy Chinese pants, but decided this hurt too much.

David wanted to take the jeep, but Pat forbade him to drive. While they were talking, David crept away and ran for the jeep like a truant schoolboy. I followed him and we jumped in.

'Are you really safe?', I asked.

'Don't worry', replied David, 'If we're going to crash — I'll stop!' He reversed out and turned then Pat sent Rick over at the double. David spotted Coco emerging from the hotel and dived into the back to reappear on my right while Pat took the wheel.

'Don't let her know I was going to drive!!'

Everyone piled in and we headed for the club. We went up to the 30th floor by express elevator. David and I were last, the manager came over to stop us. I was in my leather jacket and David wore a light V-neck pullover — no shirt. We backed off, laughing, and Pat came back and whispered in the guy's embarrassed ear.

We walked in. Everyone from the band was already celebrating at a long table. Later David and Leroy had a dance. They did the Bump, then Leroy picked him up and they both fell over a chair taking a guest with them.

Later on, I saw David leave the dance floor with a girl on his arm, then her boyfriend rushed up and took her other arm. David let her go, laughing.

After Coco and I left, they all went on to another club with a revolving floor. 'It was great', David told me, 'You could start chatting up one girl and end up with another!'

The Opening Show:- 'Fame' is David's biggest hit in the States and it finished the first half. 'We'll be back in ten short minutes,' he lied and with a wave we all disappeared off-stage. Twenty minutes later we walked out again, this time with the house lights down. Dennis started the limping drum beat of 'Five Years' (something he never got quite right) and there were shouts and cheers. Then David appeared to an ecstatic welcome — snakeskin drapecoat and huge baggy white pants. David, you look ridiculous and I love you!

And then the bombshells follow – Soul Love! Star! David dancing, bouncing, kicking – this is not Bowie posing it's David having a ball. Hang Onto Yourself! Yes, hang on. Ziggy played guitar.... a roar to this anthem. Suffragette City.... and there's an electric expectancy until WHAM, BAM, THANK YOU, MA'AM!! and as one creature the crowd leaps to its feet for this greatest single catch-phrase to the rock decade.

Tonight, and on most of the American tour, he played 'Rock 'n Roll Suicide' and as the lights came up he was there with a cigarette in his hand, a souvenir of the conceits of the past.

'What on earth can I do after Ziggy?' he had wondered one day at rehearsals.

'Has to be something to bring the energy right down – you can't top it' I said and suggested 'Art Decade'. And Art Decade it is now, with the strange coloured spots which swing around to discover the crowed. As they realise he can see them they jump up, waving, hoping to catch his eye, and a gentle little instrumental turns into a near riot.

Then followed 'Station to Station' – Roger's steam engine is so realistic you can almost see the steam and smell the sulphur. The song builds with strong piston strokes.

'It's not the side effect of the cocaine – I'm thinking that it must be love' – It is love! Every light opens up – spotlights stab, floods blaze, neon glares – white out! It nearly lifts me from my seat. 'It's too late'. It is – It's a landslide! 'It's too late' – No wonder he wanted a rock 'n roll player. 'The European cannon is here'.... is David the European cannon? Who cares – David is here. 'It's too late.... Ooohh, it's too late' The final romp, over and over, not ever wanting it to end. The guitar pizzicato, pure Fifties, tiptoes out – a quick bow and we're running off.... ●

◊ *New age "Hero"*

◊ *Sean and Rikki (right) from Boysie.*

Nicolas Roeg (signature)

Nicolas Roeg – The Jockey And The Doormat

Long before David Bowie was a face on a poster on thousands of bedroom walls all over the world, there was David Jones.

This young Londoner was possessed of two natural gifts – firstly, a sharp ear for music and the ability to write a good tune or two and secondly, an inner inclination to rise above the dreary life in the city by hamming it up. He was a natural actor and the direction in which he combined his two talents could surely have been no surprise to anyone who knew Mr. Jones before he blossomed into David Bowie.

In 1975 Bowie took his first steps to establish for himself that acting without the all-embracing mask of music was possible.

'The Man Who Fell To Earth', that strange and stimulating movie which received mixed responses when first issued and has now become a well respected and much dissected film, marked David Bowie's début performance in a major role.

The director was Nicolas Roeg, whose cinematic work has often received a similar mixture of accolades and confused sneers to Bowie's grasshopper career.

Roeg's first film to establish him as an individual to be closely watched was 'Performance' made in 1968 and co-directed by **Donald Cammell.** The film, a disorientating marriage between the cosmic ethics of permissive Sixties youth and the rigid violence of London gangsters, starred Mick Jagger.

Since then, Roeg's output has been increasingly satisfying – 'Walkabout', 'Don't Look Now', 'The Man Who Fell To Earth', Bad Timing', 'Eureka' and the latest 'Insignificance'.

Nicolas Roeg is much like the films he makes – fascinating, articulate and often frustratingly evasive. Such is the ambience of his slow and precise manner of conversation that quite often you don't realise he has avoided answering any particular question in simplistic terms. It might be more exact to say that the question loses a great deal of importance in the light of how Roeg directs the conversation.

He is among our most accomplished and innovative modern directors. He was a wise choice for David Bowie's début foray into the world of motion pictures...

♦ *Roeg performs his alchemy on the set of 'The Man Who Fell to Earth' (1975)*

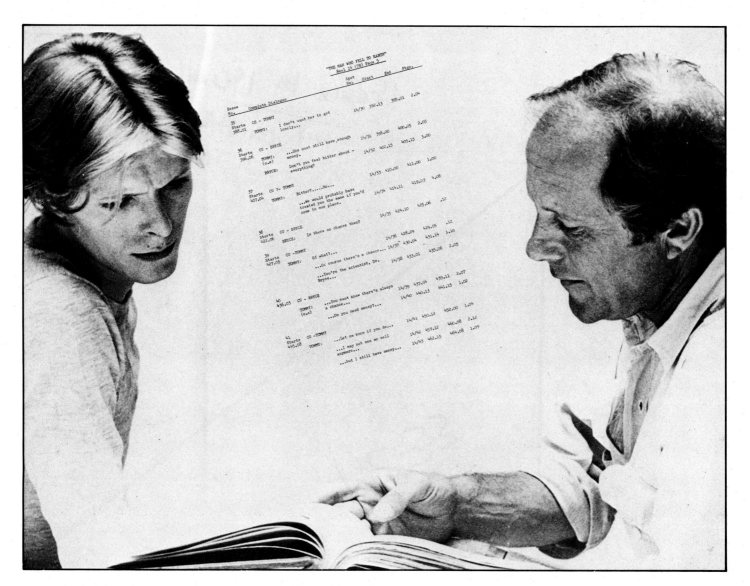

IT WAS a day of coincidences, mishappenings and attentive notice of small, teeny details that would probably, in any other set of circumstances, have gone un-noted. It's a well known compliment to Nicolas Roeg that he, as a director, investigates and displays life's details in the same way a colour-mad painter might embellish the dark red hue of a characteristic scar on a man's face more *deeply* than a photograph might. I just never expected that influence to pray on my mind before, during and after the simple act of interviewing the man. En route to the appointment, a friendly little dog, whom I would soon learn to dislike intensely, appeared to be being mistreated by his owner.

By noting this detail, my foot became acquainted with a freshly laid present he had left to Oxford Street, and the realisation that the animal was not being choked to death on the leash followed swiftly.

I had no intention of sharing my gift with a man whose work I had long since admired; those kind of joys you reserve for your worst enemies.

The next detail to be noticed was a small island of sand which suited my needs precisely. I'm not saying that small deposits of sand are unusual for Oxford Street, it's just that I never *noticed* them before.

Like I never noticed two cars of the same make, the exact same sickly green colour which surely can't be a common choice, pass each other like a folding mirror. Or, whilst playing back the recorded interview, Roeg's words would touch on to occurrences around me. The mention of the word 'doormat' the moment the television displayed an image of a man standing upon one in front of a huge castle. The doormat looked ridiculous. Sirens on the tape harmonising with sirens outside my window.

Nothing strange or unexplainable. Nothing but life.

This is the essence of Roeg's work, however – The films that carry pockets of time, that explain the lining but not the air, that itemise incidents without focusing on specific details. That cause to think, ultimately to try and rationalise, to be bemused, frustrated and above all entertained.

Two hours in Roeg's filmic company is well spent.

With my usual flair for idiotic observation, I likened his films to a good dinner. You may become familiar with the format but it's always a welcome reoccurrence. God help us if Roeg ever has the chance to film a holographic movie.

Can you *imagine*...

"The thought behind scenes in films strikes me. One that struck me tremendously was from a film made years ago called *'Greengage Summer'* which starred **Kenneth More** and **Susannah York**. There was a lovely moment in that when they're travelling across a beautiful field in France and Kenneth More in the role of this dashing young man, stops the car, turns to Susannah York and says: 'Your Mother wanted you to see a battlefield', then he points to the field, with the glorious flowers and corn, 'That's a battlefield', he concludes. The thought of that scene chilled me because I see things like that. When you visit an historical sight, you see things come alive. I take my kids to the Tower of London and say 'This is where.... That's the actual block that was used to behead Lady Jane.' They see it with great clarity. We are all astronauts of some inner time. We see that most clearly in our remembrances of things. Nostalgia is a curious thing. The word entered our language at the time of the Industrial Revolution. It means 'homesickness'.

So we know that we travel backwards with nostalgia – We sit on the sea-front at Brighton and remember holidays with parents, bucket and spade in hand.

There's a scene in 'The Man Who Fell to Earth' when the car is floating along a highway and Mr. Newton sees a group of early American settlers and some of the settlers are able to see the car. Of course, they have no conception of a car, but they see it as clearly as Mr. Newton sees them.

Now it can be postulated that Newton, as a being from another planet, possesses abilities to glimpse at such images, but Mary Lou doesn't see the settlers and most of the settlers come out too late to see the car.

In the yarn of a movie, it is a timewarp but in the thought of the scene there's a possibility of where our minds are too.

The fact is, that neither is given credence. Not the few settlers who saw the car, nor Mr. Newton who was alone in his observation. Maybe it had all been written before, maybe it hadn't. Maybe they were remembrances of the past and their shadows were able to be seen. Or maybe Mr. Newton was an astronaut of inner time. Neither would be given credence by pragmatists – people who need proof of everything. In the same sense, when I started in films, they too weren't given much credence – things like motorcars were valued and accepted more readily.

That's why I'm so glad that I began for simplistic reasons – I like film. I enjoyed going to the pictures. I believed it when someone fell from a tower. It took me a long time as a young boy to separate actors from

the roles they played, that one was only a character actor and one was the star and he couldn't order him around and so on. The great joy was believing."

Do you feel differently now, after working with film?

"No, I continue as I began. I want to believe things and the stranger the better. I guess by beginning that way I'm not drawn to the lure of 'life films' when people can say 'That's exactly Auntie Mabel' or 'That was exactly Zanzibar'. There is a place for that, but not for me. It doesn't take me anywhere – My imagination is always going further."

Nicolas Roeg does not storyboard his films, which seems as hard a task to me as putting a jigsaw together blindfolded – But perhaps I would have been disappointed if he did. 'If you put a certain amount of truth into it, it should be straightforward. And if it doesn't work then it's better to finish in truth rather than turn it into something without truth. I prefer the random quality of leaving things much more to chance.'

The chances are readily taken, the spontaneous method, the 'omen-like' area of feeling and waiting for the right moment, or idea, or occurrence are not consciously noticeable in Roeg's films. This approach does not imply a less thoughtful attitude as nothing is art for art's sake. A simple question regarding the colour of David Bowie's hair, as T.J. Newton (surely an intelligent alien would choose a less conspicuous colour, I suggested) brought forth an answer that illustrates the small details which do go unnoticed in Roeg's films. 'It suited David' would have sufficed. 'Ah yes', he replied, 'But at one point, Newton remarks 'The funny thing about television is that it doesn't tell you everything' – If you consider that his race drew all information about humans from television broadcasts then consider the possibility of untuned colour reception. I've fiddled about with the colour myself. David Owen looks vastly improved with a bright blue face!'

This brought us, rather neatly, to talk about 'The Man Who Fell to Earth' in more detail. The obvious question to open with was why cast Bowie as Newton? The 'other-worldly' aspect of Bowie's appearance is a good starter but did the initial appeal strike deeper?....

The film was written and I never cast people until the script is ready, then I sit back and ask myself 'Who are these people?' I never have the characters described, I prefer to let the scenes and interaction form the

character rather than neat descriptions.

I believe in odd omens, and there had been a BBC programme about David which I had seen ('Cracked Actor') – I remember phoning Paul (Mayersberg) who managed to catch the last few minutes. Then I obtained a tape of the programme just to look at Bowie. It wasn't his music, I guess it was his approach to life which appealed to me. It was one of the few programmes of its kind that didn't disappoint me in the person – it didn't give away the person nor did it give the impression that he was trying to be overtly secretive. He had a quality which made me interested in him. He was giving and secretive in the best possible way. He wasn't secretive for the reason of hiding something but secretive because that part of him hadn't been fully understood by himself, so as not to blurt about it until it was even vaguely understood.

After seeing the programme I was certain that David could be Mr. Newton.

I then flew to New York and we spent a long evening together talking about generalities. David had quite wisely said 'Well, let's just talk about things.' Just things. To see if we could spend months working together.

As I left, he said 'Don't worry, I'm going to do this' and I proceeded along those lines. There's not many people I would proceed with on that basis – Nothing was signed, he was under no contractual obligation but I had a sense of trust from him. People thought I was crazy – I phoned him only twice afterwards and everyone was saying 'What if he suddenly decides against doing the movie?' – But he

said 'I'll do it' with such sincerity that I totally believed in him. And then when shooting began, David arrived with a huge grin and simply said 'I told you I'd be here, didn't I?'.

It was a strength of a kind. He had made the decision. We go through life with half-arsed decisions around us. We tend to accept that promises will be broken. We look at a sense of honour in a different way.

With David the sense of honour was real, like the old days in the war when people would say 'Don't worry, I won't leave this bunker. This is the plight we're in together.'

I guess this is why some people think that David is cold. But he can't do everything for everyone. The things he says yes to he commits himself to totally."

Knowing that Bowie's great film ambition is to eventually direct himself, I wondered if Roeg was subject to a barrage of questions during the filming....

"He was always very interested but he had his part to fulfil and he was very conscious of that. He had the wit and intelligence to concentrate on his role. He wasn't a student from a film school he was the central character, but the interest was there and as we became friendly he told me that he wanted to direct films. We had a very good actor/director relationship.

The respect that had begun that night in New York. I hope that's what he felt for me because I certainly felt it for him."

Can you remember David's first comments to you on seeing the completed film?

"I remember taking a tape and that he was moved, to tears actually, but I can't remember his actual words. There was a natural embarrassment as well. 'Did we do that?' 'Do you like that' and so on. That's genuine stuff, a warmth that flows between you and your participant. Just the same as when you can tell if someone doesn't like it. 'Oh, very good. I'll call you in the morning'.

Would you like to work with him again?

"Yes I would. We have one of those pleasant friendships that has gone on without much contact. I know he knows that I watch and listen to what he's up to and I flatter myself to think that he does the same with me.

The odd times that we have met or talked again have been at the same pace. It is one of those rare associations. We have our lives to lead but we have made a mark on each other.

It would truly diminish my life if I sensed that he wasn't around any more and thinking of things.

If the time and place is right I would like to work with David again, but not to create a superficial kind of product."

How about 'The Man Who Fell to Earth' part two...?

"I have actually thought of that. About two years ago I thought about how things had changed and caught up so swiftly with what attitudes seemed to be prevailing towards a future in 'The Man Who Fell to Earth'. We had postulated that Mr. Newton would have knowledge fifteen years in advance of the world. So we had things like self-focusing, self-developing cameras where the film was more expensive than the actual camera. It took five years for those to come out after the film's release. Not fifteen, but five!!

A title struck me – I would call the film just 'On Earth'. Mr. Newton would have got out of his doldrums and he wasn't going to die because he's not a suicidal character because I believe there's hope at the end of TMWFTE. He actually says 'Of course there's hope. There's always hope.' So I thought, what would he do? He was stuck on earth forever and human knowledge would have caught up with his so he would be just a highly intelligent individual. If he didn't keep up with the world, it would eventually go that he would become rather backwards (laughs). So he would have to go out and work. Mr. Newton in the rat race!

But he would have great intelligence, great charm.... I thought he might try advertising. He would have seen the inside of business and how to market things because of his past. So 'On Earth' that's what I considered he might do."

With the plot, beginning, middle and ending rigidly defined in most other films I wondered whether Roeg was cautious/fearful/intrigued on what interpretations people (notably critics) may implant on ideas that Roeg had personally defined:

"A film is like a human being. I believe it has a life of its own. It shouldn't stop on the surface of the screen – It should go behind emotions and have some depth to it. We view all people differently 'Oh, I don't like him' or 'He's all right' but how do we really know anything? **Aleister Crowley** was thought of as a beast – It was easy to just say that. He wasn't, he was a brilliant and gentle man.

I used a quote in 'Walkabout' – Nothing could be closer than what I wanted to try and say about human beings and their relationship with the world. 'Every man and woman is a star. But what do we know of a star? By the telescope, how far it is? By the spectrascope, how bright it is? But it tells us nothing of a star.'

If a work of art, or any work, isn't open to interpretation, if it can only be one thing, the more shallow it must be. No, other people's interpretations do not worry me. I can only view them as I would view another person – 'I think they're rather splendid' or 'I don't care much for him'. I can only speak as I find. Everyone must offer themselves to the world and be truthful to themselves.

It's avoiding being put into a box and everyone tries to avoid that.

Many great plays and stories have been written around that theme. 'The Captain from Copenhagen' was about a little Jewish tailor who was sewing a Prussian officer's uniform and he decided to wear the uniform and everyone was stepping into the gutter to let him pass. When he was caught and asked why a Jewish tailor would wear a Prussian officer's uniform he replied: 'Because I didn't want to go to my maker and say that all my life I'd been a doormat' *(Cue man on TV)* People hate not knowing everything.'

Nicolas Roeg certainly doesn't tell you everything. But I don't hate him for that. He refuses to discuss his past and the why and wherefores he became attracted to film as a career, except to point out his love for the medium and the fact that decent and intelligent people never yearned for a career in the film business when he first began forty years ago.(?)

The parrot-like repetition of his life is somewhat superfluous without embarking on a biographical voyage. If you understand his words in this interview in relation to his work, then you know the titles, the content and depth of his films.

"A movie is a curious beast. The director is like a jockey on a horse. The person whose thoughts the actors refer back to is the director, much like a horse refers to the thoughts of its rider. 'Let me go', 'No I can't let you go yet because you don't know but I do, that this has got another two furlongs to go and if I let you go now you'll be too tired. But I'm glad you've told me you're ready to go, the moment you feel tired let me know also.' That's an odd analogy to make but that's about it. (laughs) It's interesting to watch things develop.

Continued on page 50.

48

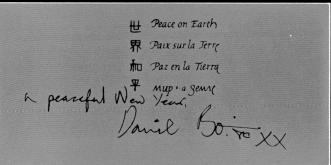

世 Peace on Earth
界 Paix sur la Terre
和 Paz en la Tierra
平 Mup : a genre

a peaceful New Year.

David Bowie xx

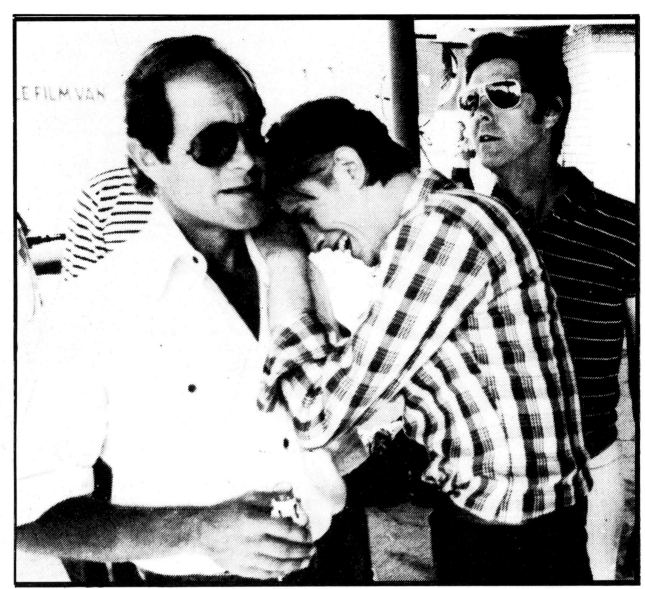

◆ *Sharing a joke on-set.*

We've all seen films where you can't quite put your finger on why they're slightly dead. You can feel the director's hand too heavy. It has nothing to do with the style of a film, it's about the internal aspect. The emotion.'

For his latest film, Roeg remarks that the 'cinema seems at its most compelling when it deals with myths. Perhaps this is because it is able, more than any other medium, to give a sense of reality. We are there. We see it happen. I believe reality surpasses our imagination and in a film we see breathing and moving before our eyes, sights we never saw in the land of our dreams. We know they are real because somewhere in our subconscious we still believe the first of all the myths of Cinema.... 'The Camera cannot lie'."

We never really wanted it to... ●

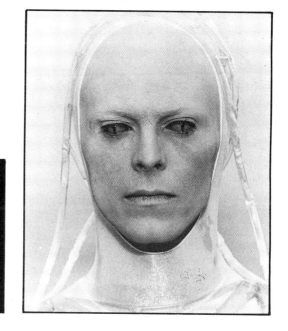

Mick Ronson – Play Don't Worry

If Hull were to one day assess its popular music successes, there would be little debate as to whether Mick Ronson should head that list. Not only has he led an active solo recording and production career, he was also the linchpin for one of the 70's most successful rock phenomena as the very basis of David Bowie's Spiders From Mars. Mick Ronson, it could be said, was a major part in Bowie's success. He is as modest about his part in the scheme of things as only he could be, reflecting a healthy stoicism rare for this business.

Mick Ronson is a native of Hull in Yorkshire, the base of his earliest R&B bands in the '60's. After a short spell at live work in London, he again returned to Hull and soon after formed his most successful local band, 'The Rats' with **Trevor Bolder** and **Woody Woodmansey**. In between times, Mick continued odd session work and travelled down to London to work on **Michael Chapman's** 'Fully Qualified Survivor' LP, which also featured the production work of **Gus Dudgeon**.

At this point in time, Bowie was preparing for a thorough onslaught on the business having rested comfortably on the fringes of success. His transient band of the moment was 'The Hype' and its drummer was **John Cambridge** — who was by good fortune a good friend of Ronson's. Cambridge suggested that Mick should make the effort to come to Beckenham and visit Bowie who was preparing a new band, and with little encouragement that is just what he did. David Bowie has always worked on an instinct with musicians. Recommendations seem to favour higher than an audition which is a trait he has carried forward to the present day. Mick Ronson was soon spearheading the Spiders from Mars, making up the rest of the numbers with the remainder of the Rats who eagerly fled Hull for the musical sanctuary of Haddon Hall. The scene was set for a major musical blitz on the world.

I met up with my first guitar hero on a sweaty August evening at a recording studio in deepest Westbourne Grove. Mick was finishing off a session for **One The Juggler**, but even after a gruelling day behind the console he was as active and alive as if the session was still young. I suppose I had expected to find the Mick Ronson image of 1973/74 — the peroxide guitar superstar —the fact was, I was greeted by a very modest, polite and together .... normal guy.

27th December, 1969

Australia 15c; New Zealand 15c; Rhodesia 2/-; West Africa 1/6; East Africa 2s.00; South Africa 15c; Malaysia 75c; Malta 1/4; Sverige SKr. 1.50 inkl moms; Deutschland Dm 1.00; Norge Kr. 2.00; Nederland Fl. 1.05; Danmark Kr. 2.60; Finland Fm 1.20; Canada 35c; U.S.A. 35c; Italia 300 lire.

Fabulous 208

1'7'208

MARMALADE STAR IN FAB'S OWN FULL~COLOUR SHOW!

PANTOMONEUM

What the stars can expect...present~wise

FEEL FESTIVE THE SCAFFOLD WAY!

Californian Christmas
Double page colour...WAYNE MAUNDER

LUXEMBOURG PROGRAMMES 23rd·29th DECEMBER

David and Angela pictured for a rare photographic modelling session.

Wishing you
a cool yule!
Love on, Bowie
XX

MGM

hunger

Melody Maker

JULY 1, 1972　　7p weekly　　USA 50 cents

LED ZEPPELIN
— the forgotten giants?

AN OUTSPOKEN INTERVIEW FROM NEW YORK
See page 24

WINTER'S COMING

EDGAR WINTER'S new White Trash are likely to appear at the next Crystal Palace concert on July 29. The band are flying in specially for the appearance—their first in Britain since 1970.

The original White Trash following their last double album "Roadwork", but former guitarist Rick Derringer will be coming over with the band, and is likely to jam with them.

Mingus due

CHARLES MINGUS will bring his sextet into Ronnie Scott's, London, to play from August 1 to 12. With the bassist will be Lonnie Hillyer (trumpet), Bobby Jones (tenor), Charlie McPherson (alto), John Foster (piano) and Roy Brooks (drums).

Another firm booking for the club is a Guitar Festival which runs from August 28 to September 23. Barney Kessel and Paco Pena are the stars for the first two weeks, then Kessel stays on and shares the bill with guitar virtuoso John Williams.

Move/ELO split?

A MYSTERY blew up over the future of the Electric Light Orchestra and The Move on Tuesday.

Reports suggest that Roy Wood has decided to leave both groups and form a new one, while Bev Bevan and Jeff Lynne will contine with ELO and the Move.

Harvest Records, the group's label, say an announcement will be made at a press conference due to be held at EMI in London tomorrow (Friday).

* The man most likely to has gone and done it, just as we predicted when we front-paged him back in January.

"The Rise And Fall of Ziggy Stardust", David Bowie's new album, has jumped into the MM chart at 19. His current tour of Britain is pulling in all the boys and girls.

A thousand people had to be turned away from Croydon's Greyhound on Sunday. See Caught In The Act on page 28.

OSIBISA
in Band Breakdown
See page 30

Courtesy Melody Maker

Like most people, I had rather lost touch with Ronson's activities of late and was eager to catch up with things. I opened with the obvious, 'What have you been up to recently?'

"Well, what I've been doing lately is …. working on this project in New York with this girl called **Sandy Dillon** — who's a pianist/singer and I've just decided to spend some time back in England, see my parents and just get around back in London again. I want to see what's going on and see people again — I haven't been back for such a long time."

Does this mean, I asked, that he was going to be back for a while now?

"I'd like to, I'd just like to spend more time over here, it all depends on what I set myself out to do."

"I have been writing too, I've been writing a lot more just lately, I have my own studio at home and I've actually been writing a lot of instrumental stuff."

So, it sounds as if you have stock-piled a lot of new material then?

"I have over a period of time, a lot of it I've thrown away. Yes, I've quite a lot of material here and there, I just haven't done much with it. But it's just for my own personal satisfaction I guess. I would like to put it out on an album one day. Much of the writing I do now is really just for my own interest, it's not like I set out and write something for an audience. I don't think of how many people it will reach, I just write it because it is just

what I want to do. If other people like it, they like it, you know …."

Is that the way you've always worked, or did you write the first two solo LP's for the public or for yourself?

"Well, those first albums were just something that I did at the time, nothing else."

When your second solo LP came out, were you preparing for another one to follow?

"No, no. At that point in time I was ready to forget the whole thing. I didn't really know why I was doing it. I didn't have a particular reason why I should be a 'vocal' artist, as it were. I'm more of an instrumentalist, more of a musician than I am a singer you see. I can sing one or two songs that I really believe strongly in singing but to be a singer …. I'm not. I'm a musician and that's what I was really meant to do, and that is what I am best at doing. I don't want to be a singer and I don't want to be known as a singer, that has nothing to do with me at all."

Would you like the material you have stock-piled to be released at all in the future?

"Yes I would, because even though the material may have been written over the past two or three years, it still holds up for me, it sounds as strong as when I did it. It's sort of timeless, and I think that that is the true test when something is timeless.

When something sounds just as good three years on, whereas if you just follow the latest trend it sort of goes out of fashion really, and you're sort of lumbered with it, and you don't know what to do with it. I think, the real thing is for it to be playable in any year, and it still sounds valid and really good. So that's the kind of thing I'm after really."

Are you actually making efforts to do that at all?

"I do make an effort now and again, I don't go out and make a whole concentrated effort — I like doing production too, you see. I have approached one or two record companies in the past about putting out material but they all want the immediate single …. and I can't guarantee them an immediate single, not for what I do."

Could you ever become part of a group again?

"I think I could, but not for ever and a day I think just for general experience. But the group thing is not what I am searching for, but I would like to play again. I would

58

definitely like to go out and play, as an involvement thing with other people. It's not like I need to do it for my own 'trip' or anything, be my whole personal project, it would be to just get together with other musicians and to produce something people would enjoy listening to."

If you became part of a band again, could you do another world tour like the ones you were doing in 1973?

"Oh yeah, sure. If it was good music and something I was really enjoying doing, of course I would."

It wasn't too much of a drag for you, that kind of discipline?

"No, not at all, they were enjoyable, real enjoyable."

Your first and only solo tour didn't seem to go too happily for you at the time, what do you think went wrong with it?

"Well, it was sort of being bamboozled out of the last David Bowie concert and approached with the offer that I could be the next David Cassidy or whoever it may be, do an album right now and sort of being real impressionable as I am I sort of went with it, and I thought it was a real good idea. It's something that I think everybody would like to do, and I just happened to do it. While I was on the road, and started to play that material, I started to think to myself, 'Is this right for me, why am I doing this? I don't really feel that comfortable doing this, it's not really one hundred per cent me. I'm sort of fooling myself, and I'm not only fooling myself, I'm fooling other people too.' So I found that I was starting to feel very uncomfortable within myself. By that, I knew that other people would spot that in the audience and I didn't want that, I didn't want to carry on with that any more. Because you have to feel very confident in yourself and if you don't feel that confident in yourself, how are you going to come across to other people. I initially felt that doubt in rehearsals really, I was thinking, 'Hey, wait a minute, I can't wait to finish this'. I just couldn't wait to get it over with, in a way. Everything kind of happened in such a rush, I just got very confused, it just all happened so quickly that I didn't have time to work it out or why I was doing it. I think the main reason was, why I was doing it, more than what I was doing ...."

I think the history books show just how hard you were working at the time, and the fact that your albums that came out of that period show just how well you could

handle that kind of situation, because they have lasted well and they are good LP's and don't sound rushed ....

"Well, that's because I didn't want to be pushed into putting out bad material. Although that whole period wasn't such a bad thing, it wasn't quite right either which wasn't only my fault or anybody's fault in particular .... it just happened."

At the time of Bowie's retirement announcement, all the Spiders seemed generally suprised about it — did you know it was going to happen or did you find out on the night?

"No, I sort of knew it was happening really. It was just something that had to happen, it

was always going to happen. I knew that it would eventually happen anyway."

Do you remember that Hammersmith show at all, was it memorable for you?

"Yeah, it was memorable, a lot of the shows were memorable but that one was especially because it was the last one in that format. We recorded right after that of course. I mean, I remember other shows well like the Kingston Polytechnic, or the London Polytechnic, Elephant and Castle. I remember the pub up in Birmingham that we played, some really small ones, a few pubs. They were pretty memorable too, I mean the whole thing was."

You seem to be generally pleased with what was achieved in the early seventies, it seems to have set a firm foundation for you ....

"Oh yeah, you bet. It was great, it was very exciting. I mean I saw the film yesterday, only yesterday (the farewell show), I saw it for the first time and I thought it was really

exciting, I thought it was quite something."

Do you feel that you were good friends with Bowie at the time, or was he distant?

"No, not really, we got on all right .... we got on real good. You have your ups and downs don't you, everybody does. No, I think we all got on really good together."

The history of the recording of 'The Man Who Sold The World' is quite interesting in that it is generally known that both you and Tony Visconti helped to save that particular recording due to David's troubles at the time. Did you feel that you were fairly credited?

"I don't know really, I can't remember. I thought I was treated fairly in a lot of ways."

Do you remember your very first meeting with him?

"Oh yeah, in his flat, we just sat around in his flat. I picked up a guitar and jammed with him. He said 'Hey, do you wanna come down to this radio show and play with me ....' So we went down to this radio show and I played along with him. After that he said, 'Well, how about coming along and playing with me all the time ....' So I agreed, and that was pretty much straight after the show. He said something like, "How about going back to Hull, packing your bags and coming down to work with me', that was about it. So I did and came down to live in Haddon Hall."

Didn't you have to rough it on the landing for a while?

"No, we had our own room for a long while. When the house was being decorated and things like that we had to sleep on the landing, but that was all right, a bed's a bed isn't it?"

Were you aware of his work before you came down to meet him?

"No, not really."

Do you find that things from that period in time become cloudy in your memory?

"Not really, it's quite clear to me .... everything is, I've a pretty good memory."

*The radio show referred to earlier by Mick was a BBC 'In Concert' for John Peel's 'The Sunday Show'. The performance was recorded at the Paris Cinema studio in Lower Regent Street on February 5th 1970 and broadcast on the 8th. Listening back to that show now, it's amazing to think that Mick had only met David the day before. The set was generally acoustic but it took Ronson only a short time to find his feet and add some familiar guitar accompaniment. The tracks they played on Peel's show were; '**Amsterdam**'/'**God Knows**'*

59

Continued on page 62

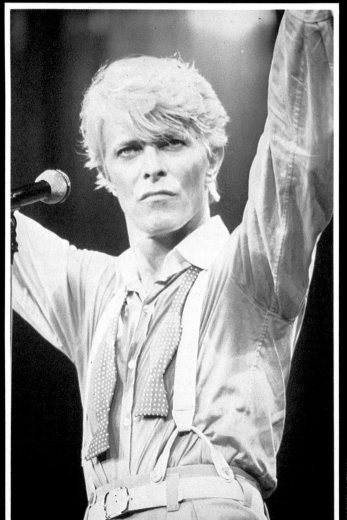

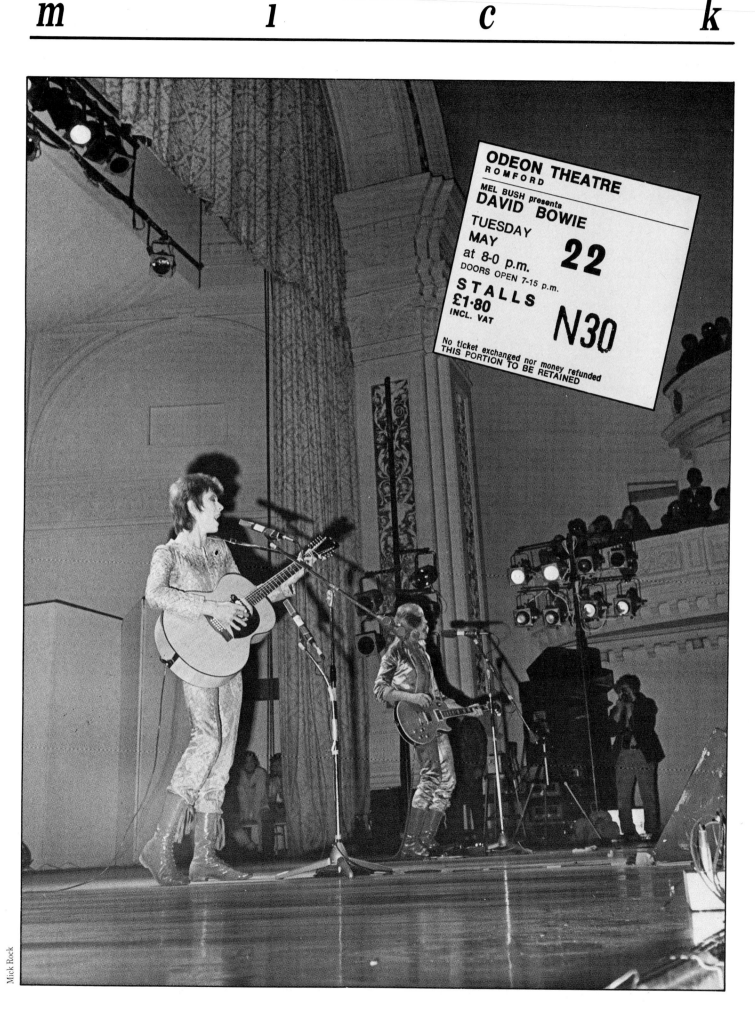

Mick Rock

I'm Good'/'London Bye Ta Ta'/'An Occasional Dream'/'The Width Of A Circle'/'Janine'/'Wild Eyed Boy from Freecloud'/'Unwashed and Somewhat Slightly Dazed' and 'The Prettiest Star'.

I asked Mick, having only known of David Bowie for just 24 hours, how he managed to accompany him on a concert recording?

"I didn't know anything, none of the material, I just sat and watched his fingers. I didn't really know what I was doing, but I suppose it came across OK, I don't know? Maybe it sounded horrible, I really don't know. Everybody seemed to like it though, I'll have to listen to your cassette of it, I'd love to hear that."

Was that treated as an audition, the radio performance?

"I don't know if it was an audition or not, I never really thought of it like that. I was just playing, it was a normal thing for me .... It probably was an audition, who knows?"

Did you feel at the time that David Bowie was rather weird?

"Not at all, I thought he was a very nice gentleman".

*At this point, I got out a copy of **Ken Pitt's** book to read the passage of Ken's account of Mick's first meeting with David. **John Cambridge's** account to Ken was very concise and exacting and Mick regularly retorted, 'That's right ....' after each sentence. The piece about meeting David first at the Marquee did rather confuse him as he, as has been stated already, thought the first meeting came at Haddon Hall, Mick continues;*

"Well, that could have been right. I do remember the Marquee, but I thought that came after .... that may well be right. I was all a bit confused then simply because I was too busy worrying what I was going to do for the show. The broadcast recording was in front of a live audience too, so it was just like a regular show, and I just had to play ...."

John Cambridge was obviously quite instrumental with your introduction to Bowie, do you still keep in touch with him now?

"No, I haven't seen him for a long, long time. He's a funny lad though, real comical. He used to make me laugh all the time, a really nice bloke."

Did you work much in the basement studio at Haddon Hall?

"Well, the basement was sort of put up a little later on, we didn't use it much. It was just too small. You had to go down these dark tiny stairs into this little basement to this tiny, tiny room. We didn't use it much, we started rehearsing upstairs .... the piano was up there, the amps were set up there."

So much of David's most important early material was thought out and written there, you must have felt quite a part of it all ....

"I did, it was all very important to me. It was a really interesting period for me. I was just learning so much in so little time, all at once. There was all this stuff that I had never been exposed to before that was all brand new to me. It was really enjoyable, fantastic. I was lucky because I was allowed to do what I wanted, which I thought was really good of David. He gave me a lot of freedom which gave me the chance to express myself as well. That was all good for me .... that was a good quality he had."

Did you get to know Tony Visconti well at that time?

"Yes, I did, very well. I don't see him now. I used to go to the studio and watch him working. He used to let me watch him mixing and working out arrangements, I used to think it was amazing what he used to do. I used to help him and copy out pieces, it was great for learning. I did the strings on Life on Mars".

Did that come about from watching Tony Visconti working?

"That's right. I thought that if he could do it, then I could do it too. I can read and write music, after playing classical piano, violin and everything, it was just an extension of that. Learning classical music for me was a great help in that area, but at the same time I felt that it also hindered me a bit too. In classical music everything has to be relative, for example, the relative minor to a C chord is A minor and when you are brought up on classical rules you tend to follow them. You end up playing by the rules because they are so strict and forced into you. So, in some ways, classical training was a very good thing for me to go through, but in other ways I wish I had never known anything about classical music at all. It still affects the way I think now."

Do you remember when David used to collect antiques, did that interest you?

"He used to say, 'Let's go out and look at some antique shops', which really didn't interest me. I was never interested in antiques myself. He never used to do all that too much, just now and again shop for them. He used to come back and say 'Look at this I've just bought, isn't it wonderful ....' I used to think that it looked like a piece of garbage to me, all black and rusty. I don't appreciate antiques too much myself."

Home for Mick these days has generally been New York, where he has a house which is complete with its own studio. His wife, Sue Ronson, is the lady who used to do the hair for David and the Spiders in 1973.

The reunion... Mick Ronson and David Bowie in 1983...

"I was working in Toronto at the time and I found out that David was playing there. I just called up Corrine Schwab and got some tickets and went along to the show. David said to me, 'Why don't you play?'. So I said, No, no, I can't play. I don't want to do that. 'So, later on, after the show he said, why don't I come and play tomorrow night. I said I couldn't because I was working, I was in the studio. Anyway, the following night came along and we had been working all afternoon and I thought, 'Sod it, let's go down to the show. So we all went down to the show and he said, 'Well, are you going to play tonight?' and I said, 'All right, I'll play'. We did '**Jean Genie**' I think. I did enjoy it, it was great. I was playing through an amp I didn't know though and the stage was very big. I was playing **Slick's** guitar and I couldn't hear where my sound was coming from. I had heard Slick play solos all night so I decided not to play solos and I just went out and thrashed the guitar.

I really thrashed the guitar, I was waving the guitar above my head and all sorts of things. It was funny afterwards because David said, *(talking about Earl Slick)* 'You should have seen his face...' meaning he looked petrified. I had his prize guitar and I was swinging it around my head and Slick's going 'Waaaa..watch my guitar', you know. I was banging into it, and it was going round my head. Poor Slick. I mean, I didn't know it was his special guitar, I just thought it was a guitar, a lump of wood with six strings. Later on I found it was his special guitar.

Anyway, we had a good chat, it was the first time I had seen him for a real long time..."

We parted, promising to meet up again to finish off the hundred thousand other questions I never asked, Mick heading for Bromley where he was temporarily staying. ●

suits

you ....

George Simms – Singing Serious

So you're on-stage, standing next to your brother and this English rock star starts singing these catchy little tunes in front of thousands of people and you join in, careful not to lose your hat or ruffle your striped suit.

Soon, you're travelling all over the planet with this tousle-haired Londoner and the next thing you know — he's got you singing on his albums and introducing his shows in all kinds of funny languages.

How does all this happen? What sequence of events creates such a situation? And, just as importantly, how does it feel?

1983 was the Bowie blitz year, in which the wolfish loner returned to the pack aiming to steal his way into young people's hearts (*'I never knew I'd need so many people'*) – For the most part, he succeeded, and ripped any traces of cult from his name replacing it with a label he'd previously gone to any cost to avoid – 'pop star'.

George Simms, one of the backing vocalists on 'Let's Dance', 'Tonight' and the Serious Moonlight tour, recalls some random moments from the megatour that gave David Bowie to the world – or vice versa....

♦ *'Take your coat, sir?' DB pictured with George Simms.*

◊ *Union City Jack.*

◊ *Scene from 'The Hunger' that never actually made the final print.*

Greg Gorman

◆ *Serious sophistication.*

GEORGE SIMMS comes from a very musical family that raised him and his two brothers, Frank and Stephen, in the South Western part of America.

His father worked successfully as a radio and television presenter and his Uncle Hank also enjoyed a flourishing career in the media — his voice being known the world over as the deep, resounding tones behind the yearly Oscar award ceremony and various television programme introductions.

From a very early age, the young Simms brothers were exposed to music of all kinds and encouraged to sing within the family unit.

One story illustrates the strange, almost telepathic link between George and his brother Frank. One night, when they were young, their mother caught them singing the same song in complete harmony with one another. Both were sound asleep in their beds at the time.

Together, the Simms brothers continued to exercise their vocal inclinations, forming with local groups and entertaining people at high school dances, performing a mixture of Motown and surfing styles of music.

In 1971, a phone call from an old school friend **David Wolff** set into motion a chain of events that led to a meeting with **Dave Spinner,** with whom, and after working on

various projects with Wolf that failed to break, they developed a vocal style that led the three of them to continue to write and sing together.

Their first professional job was backing **Harry Chapin** on his single 'Cat's In The Cradle' which was a number one hit in the States.

After doing more work with Chapin and regularly singing in New York cafés they gained a healthy reputation and added others to their line-up to become a fully-fledged band — The Simms Brothers.

Two albums issued on Elektra suffered due to lack of promotion from the record company despite the top quality producers (**Mike Stone and Eddie Kramer**) involved in their creation.

From there on, regular session work followed, and having added a keyboard player who previously worked with **Chic, Nile Rodgers** and **Bernard Edwards** attended a few of their gigs and enlisted their talents to any projects they were working on.

December 1982 and George and Frank Simms had just finished work on Nile Rodgers' solo album 'Adventures In The Land Of The Good Groove' when Rodgers phoned them to say: "Hey, I've got another project for you guys, if you're interested — It's David Bowie."

George takes up the story from there:

"We turned up at the studio. Nile was there with an engineer. He said 'OK, this is what the first song sounds like'. He had a few lines scribbled down and without giving us a range of notes or any particular flavour that he wanted, we just sung the song in a way that sounded good to us and he said 'Hey, that's it — Let's go in and record it'.

About halfway through recording the song, this guy with a hat walked in and sat down in a corner of the control room. We went through to listen to the playback, still without being introduced to David. He was sitting by the window, and after a few seconds when our parts came up, he drew closer to us and suddenly said, 'That's great!'. So, without any formal introductions, that's how we got to know David. I guess he's reasonably shy in front of people he's never met before, but having heard our work and being excited enough that it suited his style, we were friends. On that day, we worked for six hours then came back on the Sunday to work another three hours and, for us, that was 'Let's Dance'. I was very excited by the music.

Unfortunately, I didn't have a great storehouse of knowledge about David's career.

At the time if you'd have offered me a million dollars to name five Bowie song titles I wouldn't have been able to do it. I knew David Bowie as the artist who sang 'Ground Control To Major Tom' — that's what I would have said and that isn't even the correct title of that song!

I remember when that was released in 1969, I thought it was one of the greatest songs ever, and I used to sing along with it whenever it was on the radio. It was kind of strange to think that fifteen years later I'd be singing the same song with the man himself.

All that time in the studio there was no mention at all of a tour. We just thought that it was a job well done for a super artist and maybe one day he'll call us again.

Then the tour was announced and we thought, 'Nah, it couldn't possibly happen' but it did, David called us and asked if we'd like to join the band!

At this point, his office sent us both a tape of songs that we should become familiar with. As I listened I heard so many songs that I had loved for years without ever realising it was Bowie. I couldn't wait to sing them on stage."

What did you do the day before such a huge tour opened?

"I remember that I scoured every shop in Brussels looking for a pair of outrageously ugly eyeglasses. We had rehearsed the 'Cracked Actor' routine and I wanted the glasses to play a joke on David during the final rehearsal. David has a very good sense of humour — You can pull any stunt on him and as long as it's in good taste he'll enjoy it as much as anyone. So I eventually found the glasses I considered ugly enough, pulled the stunt and he cracked up during 'Cracked Actor'."

The costumes that the band members wore were dictated down to the smallest detail. George was happy with his sedately striped suit, except for the hat which, being light and floppy, often got lost in the crowd or flattened like a pancake in transit between shows. Two sets of the costumes were made and worn alternately — one set was given to each member as mementos of the tour. The opening night came — What were the band's feelings?'

It was so important — working for an artist who has such a fantastic reputation. None of us wanted to let David down, not because there was the feeling that any axe would fall.

EMI

There was never, ever that feeling on the tour. David had made it abundantly clear, not so much in words but in his attitude, that he had hired each of us because he had faith in our abilities. So we didn't want to let him down because in addition to being such a major star he's also a major great person."

As the Serious Moonlight tour wound its way across many countries, George would use any free time by exploring cities, sight-seeing and soaking up the varied cultures around him. **Earl Slick** *would often accompany him, leaving most of the other band members still sleeping in their hotel rooms after late nights on the town.* "Slicky would call me up early and we'd be out". *By using his extensive knowledge of languages, George encountered very few problems in communicating with people.*

Prior to the start of the tour, George and Frank Simms spent an enormous part of the three weeks spent in Dallas rehearsing with

just Bowie. The majority of stage moves were all carefully choreographed to fit snugly with the settings of the computer vari-lights. One song that originally appeared on the rehearsal song list that never actually got to rehearsal stage was 'Across The Universe'. I asked George to describe Bowie's working methods, a question that often comes to mind during SZ interviews and one which always receives a similar response:

"What seems like a dichotomy. At times he would be deadly serious, because this was his career and the way he presents himself to the public, but at the same time it was very loose and very, very happy. Frank and I both have very way-out senses of humour, along with David's, and we would often change lyrics and song titles to make them sound funny. Like instead of 'Red Sails' it would be 'Dead Snails' and 'We Can Be Heroes' became 'We can be Negroes', 'Breaking Glass' often became 'Breaking Wind' (laughs) and David loved it!

♦ *Million dollar scrawls.*

♦ *Arriving in Japan (1980).*

He's enough of a professional to realise that when you're working such huge blocks of hours, the more levity and personal interaction you have brings you all closer together."

Did you all read the reviews much?

"Oh, yes, and of course most of them were very complimentary. For myself and Frank, we were very gratified to read that most reviews had noted our presence favourably, that we were able to work up front on stage with David without up-staging him. We didn't let the bad press get us down either. There was one review, I think it was from Australia, that cut up everyone in the band including David. It said things like David is horrible and should have been a railway conductor, Earl Slick has lost a lot of weight around his waistline and gained it in his head — Frank and George Simms are the most annoying thing on four legs ever seen — I mean, who should get upset over a stupid review such as that?

Still on the subject of reviews, one day in Berlin, David called me up to his hotel room because we had planned to go to the Brücke Museum which displays a lot of early 20th Century Expressionist painters like **Heckel** who is David's favourite. David pointed out a large wood-block print by Heckel, that of a man with an angular green face. He leaned over to me and whispered 'I have the same print at home, but mine's better'. In his room he said 'Oh, George have you seen the Berlin review?'. I said that I hadn't so he handed me the paper. As I read it I could see David watching me with this twinkle in his eye. I got up to the part 'David Bowie is supported admirably by Frank and Joyce Simms'. He was just waiting, biting his lip and trying not to laugh until I got to the Joyce part.

Another night in the dressing room before the show, Frank and I had been laughing about **John Candy** who's a performer on Second City Television in the States and one of his characters is 'Mr Mambo'!!! He wears a silk tuxedo, ruffled shirt and a perpetual silly grin as he does the Mombo. So, laughingly, we mentioned to David that it would be funny if we all went on doing the Mombo walk, silly grin and all. This night, as he came to introduce us he said 'My backing vocalists — The Mambo brothers!' and we strode up to the front of the stage doing 'Mr Mambo'! We all had a good laugh and so did David, then later as we came back on for the encores, David, in full view of the audience, came back on doing this same silly walk. That was the feeling, everything was loose and fun and David set the tone for that."

From 1983 we continued into 1984 to talk about the recording of 'Tonight' on which George was present but his brother was not:

"Frank was asked to but he had already agreed to sing on **Billy Joel's** tour prior to the call from David's office. David said that we could choose the singer to replace Frank, just for that album, and without a moment's hesitation we chose **Curtis King** who we'd worked with on all the Nile Rodgers projects. So we drove to Montreal and the day we arrived David invited us up to the big house where we had these luxurious 8 or 9 course meals every night. After the meal, David said 'If you guys aren't too tired we can do a song tonight' so we went in and recorded 'Blue Jean'. The next day we did another four hours, the day after that was off, following that we worked from early evening to 2.00am and that was the album.

I think David was happy with Curtis. I think he regretted the chance not to work with Frank again but was happy with the way things worked out. After the album was finished, David invited me to stay for another eight days as his guest.

During that time I got to know **Iggy Pop** very well, he's great. It's no wonder that the two of them are so close as they are so similar — Both frighteningly intelligent, well versed in world affairs and both great fun.

David was such a gracious host and I really appreciate the fact that he invited me to stay because I met so many talented people involved in the recording of that album, and because we were so isolated there was no pressure from fans or whatever. Iggy and I would take long walks together and the air was so fresh. It was a very relaxing way to record an album.

I've heard that he's writing new material so I guess that means another album is on the way. *(Bowie still has three more albums and three years in which to deliver them on his EMI contract).* David doesn't really announce his intentions ahead of time. It's really a matter of waiting until he's ready to move on something. Of course, we're all so crazy about that guy that as soon as he does, we'd drop anything to work with him again. For my personal projects — Frank has a writing partner Mickey Leonard who have a great song-writing ability as a team. We often get together to record songs, so that is an ongoing situation. For other work as backing vocalists, we generally have about two or three days notice, so we just take them as they come, hoping that they won't preclude us from anything David's doing. Number one, I look at David as a friend, number two as a fellow musician who's asked me to work with him and number three as the great, untouchable star. To know David is to put them in the order of priorities as stated – a friend, a fellow musician and the greatest star ever.

Another incident I can recall involves the routine in 'Cracked Actor' where I would place the glasses on David just before he went into the song. Some nights it was difficult for me to see where the top of his ear was, because of his hair or whatever and I would hit with one ear and miss the other. One night in the dressing room in Gothenburg, we were all in a crazy mood and I was joking with David about the many different permutations of what could go wrong with the glasses so when it came to do the actual show I was really on my toes and determined to get it right.

So that night I came up to David, very serious, holding the glasses correctly and he was going already. His lips were quivering, I guess he was remembering the laugh we had back-stage, he was trying very hard not to break down in laughter.

Still deadly serious, I held the glasses near his face, thinking 'He's not gonna affect me – He's not going to make me laugh'. I was trying so hard to get it right I held the glasses too tightly and, by accident, let go of one of the bows – It caught David right in the eye!

The audience must have thought he'd gone crazy. He couldn't sing the song at all and it took him until 'Ashes to Ashes' to finally calm down. And I was very much the same...."

The interview was also very much the same – with much laughter and zest. George Simms is a likeable man with a distinct flair for story-telling that perhaps loses a great deal between the translation to print. (If only we could bring you his visual depiction of 'Mr Mambo'!).

George recently recalled other fractured song titles – 'Scary Dinners' instead of 'Scary Monsters' (a comment on the sometimes unpredictable quality of the catered food) 'My Wife's On Mars' instead of 'Life On Mars', 'White Mice' for 'White Light' and 'Fat People' in place of 'Cat People'.

The striped suit is no more, but the dance goes on forever... ●

♦ *To — ni — ght!*

B L A C K O U T

Lindsay Kemp – Flighting The Fantasy

To describe a Lindsay Kemp show is to describe the well-thumbed pages of a child's picture book, or that transient moment, experienced by adults and children alike, between waking and sleeping when the mind's images congeal to create a wonderland that Alice would have been proud of.

To describe the man himself is much harder. A dictionary of descriptions have already been given, each as confused as the other.

Coming from Liverpool (despite telling the world for many years that he originated from Scotland), his progression is charted by art school, mime studies with **Marcel Marceau** and dance training with **Marie Rambert**.

After founding his first company in 1962, Kemp's diverse theatrical experience included directing Soho strip-tease to one-man shows and creating original ballets for the Ballet Rambert.

Today, successfully touring the world with his present company, Kemp is regarded as one of the leading exponents of mime and dance, and now returns to England regularly for well received performances.

Kemp first met David Bowie in the summer of 1967 and briefly instructed him on the benefits of mime applied to any theatrical presentation.

Their associations together produced many new and exciting ideas and influences for the young Bowie who has since remarked 'I owe it all to Lindsay'.

Despite highly conflicting reports on how much Kemp actually did teach Bowie (Kemp maintains that Bowie studied with him for three years, while others close to Bowie at the time offer a much different picture by saying that Bowie only actually attended a few weeks' worth of lessons) it is certain that, one way or another, Lindsay Kemp directed Bowie's flair for theatrics and encouraged him to combine his music and theatre together in a form that would eventually take great importance on Bowie's later career....

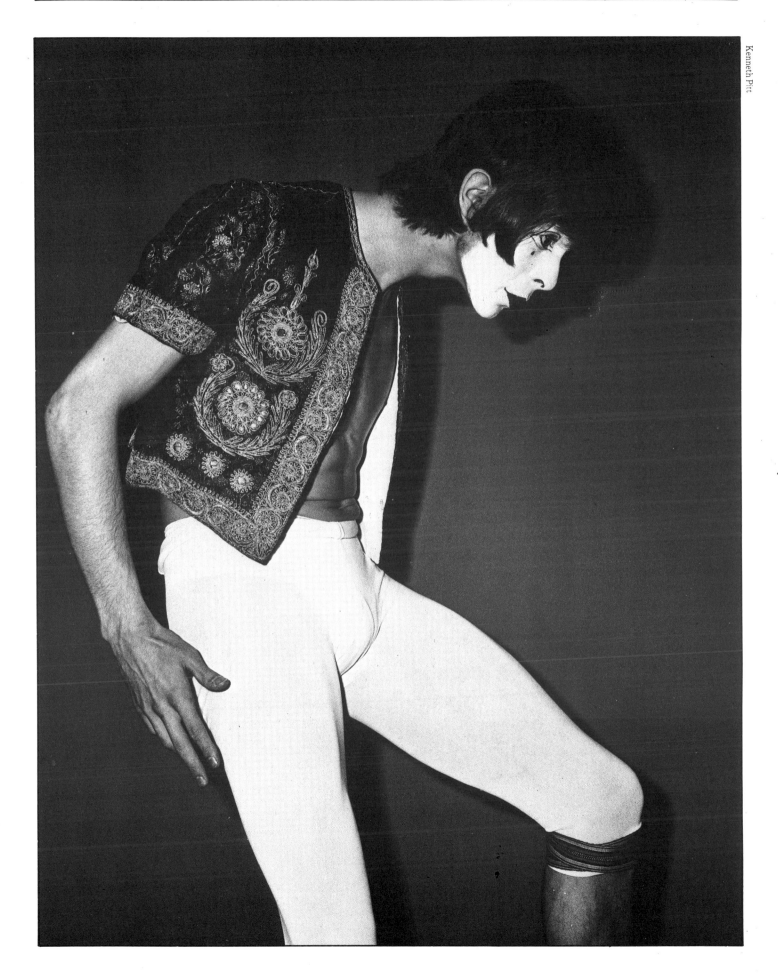

*One of the rarest Bowie books —
Issued 1972.*

Bow — ie.

Cover star.

How long have you been publicly performing mime?

"I've never performed mime. I'm not a mime. I'm a dancer. When David Bowie came to me I taught him to dance — that is, to be. To celebrate his life and encourage other people to do the same. To dance is to let one's spirit escape."

Was dance always your chosen vocation, even as a child?

"Well, yes! The same as you, the same as everyone here in the bar. All children dance, being fabulously spontaneous abandoning themselves to the laws and desires of nature. It's only later on when parents and teachers stifle us and make us like everyone else — everything that's safe and un-noticed. Dance is expression and communication, an embrace for our brothers as God intended. Flowers never stand in isolation unless they've been cultivated and tainted by sophisticated gardeners. Everything that God intended is an embrace with other aspects of nature. The wave dancing with the moon, the wave dancing with the drowning sailor. One person at the end of the bar smiling at the person at the other end. The way that Bowie sings, not in isolation, but sharing rhythms with the heartbeats of his public. There is no such thing as a secret dancer. Nature doesn't have any secrets. The English have secrets which is why I didn't like it here very much. They conceal things. Secretness is boring. We should be entertaining people all the time. To do that is to encourage love — not all this punching and violence."

You once said that everyone is born with genius. Is the extent of that genius the same in everyone?

"To begin with, yes. Some of us have more courage than others, some of us are less selfish. Genius can also be selfish. But the great genius's like the genius of **Picasso** or **Shakespeare** or **Isadora Duncan** is a very generous thing. It's an appeal for everyone to stop killing each other."

What is your fondest memory of Bowie?

"The first time I slept with him, I suppose. No, the first time I ever saw him. (pauses in thought) No — The first time I heard him on the radio. It's all so fabulously confused. I heard him on the radio and it sounded exactly the way that I would sing if I had that kind of voice. My voice, of course, is my gestures, my body. I identified with Bowie, the same way I identified with **Jean Genet** or **Picasso.** The voice attracted me like a siren. I was Ulysses

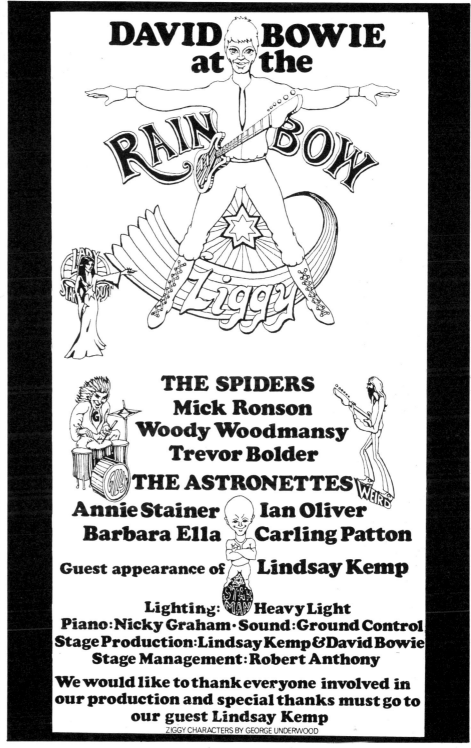

attracted by the song of Sertee. No-one else had heard of him and I used to go around to the nearest record store and say 'Hey! You got any David Jones?' (laughs). And when I first saw him standing in the doorway, I never expected him to look anywhere near as attractive as he sounded because they hardly ever do. It's like the soldiers during the war — they were all in love with Vera Lynn and then they saw her and were terribly disappointed.

The people you meet that look fantastic and talk to you about their records or paintings, when you see or hear them they turn out to be absolutely awful. What was so wonderful about David Bowie was that he looked every bit as marvellously as he sang, and all I really did for him was to make him look a little more striking.

I gave him a visual beauty that he didn't have before. At the beginning, like any new love, you want everyone to notice — 'Who's that maaan I saw you with last night' — It's very important, especially for me, that they notice what I'm wearing or who I am in love with. But they didn't mention him. They didn't mention his voice, they didn't mention the way he looked. So I picked up a tin of red spray paint and I sprayed his hair red and then they noticed.*

When he became successful, I was overwhelmed by it. I was living in Scotland and Bowie had been in London for six months and it was extraordinary. In six months he had become acclaimed. We did the Ziggy Stardust show at the Rainbow together. We wrote a lot of those songs for each other. It was the first time they were talking about Gay Rock."

Did you expect his career to go any differently than it did?

"Well, he constantly surprises us. He is the divine chameleon. He changes his colours all the time and frequently for the better. No, I am surprised. The same as you are surprised, the same as his public is surprised, the same as his poor mother is surprised, and the same as he himself must be surprised. That he can allow so much of his heart and imagination to escape so marvellously."

Will you ever work together again?

"Well, I look forward immensely to when we do work together again. Of course, we are planning to do a retrospective world tour together. That's the possible future. But I don't like talking about the past. It's hard for me to even talk about last night's performance. There were a lot of joyful moments with Bowie but also a great deal of agony."

How would you best like to be remembered?

"I'd like to think that I made people smile and that those people have helped other people to smile. I'm really only here to encourage joy. There's no life without joy, you know. Occasionally in my work we're among the people of the agony and suffering and if I can make them smile it's worthwhile."

Have you noticed any changes in London?

"The English persist in being the most wonderfully optimistic pessimists!! They are still optimistic even though they have a demon in power. The English ought to kick more people up the ass than they do. To be more of themselves, to retain that politeness because good manners are extremely

essential. Now I think the English are admitting their mistakes by coming to see me in performance. Seven years ago I did play to almost empty houses.

I'm also an optimistic pessimist — It's got to get better as it's at its lowest ebb. But I'm here, struggling away on the stage, to try and get people to STOP driving those trucks with bombs aiming to blow people up. I'm appalled and extremely saddened by the state of the world but I'm going on-stage tonight and I'll do my bit."

You studied with Marcel Marceau — What was the single greatest thing he taught you?

"He gave me my hands. Before Marcel, my hands were like strawberry-coloured boxing gloves. He restored my hands, he performed

♦ *Lindsay Kemp*   Gina Coyle

on the ends of my arms the most remarkable plastic surgery. Before, I was obliged to box for survival not only with my boxing gloves but also with my feet and eyes. In other words, I became an entertainer. Not only because I needed the money or that I enjoyed dancing but also as a means of protecting myself against the blows of other boys at school, the queer bashers in the street. Marcel transformed my handless arms into butterfly wings."

He talks as though the world is his audience; flash of an eye, sweep of a hand, accentuating the words that matter. It could be a game, it could be for real, as real as the smile and the kindness and the mischief....

What is the greatest compliment that you could be given?

"I suppose that they would understand me. I don't mind them saying that they think I'm nice looking, but I wouldn't believe them (laughs). Unfortunately, I find compliments all too easy to forget. I try very hard, especially before I go on stage. I try to remember all the wonderful things that people have said about me, but I never can. Each performance for me is agonising before I go on. I'm always vomiting in the toilet and so on. Dancing as a child was so much easier."

Did you enjoy your appearance at the Bowie Convention in Hammersmith in 1983?

(Kemp was interviewed on stage in front of thousands of avid Bowie fans. A film show followed after the interview and one individual from the audience shouted out: 'When does the film start?' Undaunted, Kemp battered his eyelashes and retorted 'But darling, the film has already started.')

"No, I was terribly nervous. I hadn't been in London for years and I thought that people would think how can this bald-headed old queen have been Bowie's boyfriend? It was quite an ordeal."

Do you still paint regularly?

"All the time. Sometimes with my tongue, sometimes with my breath, my whispers". *again, the glint in the eye.*

If you had the chance to speak to everyone in the world for ten seconds — What would you say?

"All I could do in that amount of time is just present myself. I wouldn't actually say anything as people say things. But I would say a great deal, as I always do when I'm not speaking. I would BE. With sufficient confidence, not in my dancing or painting or writing but in the love that I have in my heart. I know that people would see it and understand. I've met many great people, by great I don't mean famous but great humanists. And I don't speak to them, I just allow myself to be and they instantly understand me. They know that I have the same intention."

Does it mean a lot to you when people come backstage after a show to congratulate you?

"Yes, it does. I find it extremely exhausting, though. Much more so than the actual show. To have to continue to be the energetic young dancer that was in the glare of the spotlight. I'm pleased but I always find it impossible to

* *According to correspondence from Corinne Schwab, this never happened. Although, as she admits "It makes a good story."*

♦ *with Freddi Burretti*

Mick Rock

♦ *Somewhere over the rainbow.*

♦ *This is the only picture in existence of Bowie appearing on Cairngorm Ski night　1970 — The tape has been wiped.*

admit how exhausted I am. You can never admit to being tired. Our duty is to AWAKEN the world. Take now for example, I haven't eaten for days. I was at a big do that was put on for us last night. All the lords and ladies were there. I still didn't have the chance to eat all the lovely food that had been prepared. I was being k-i-s-s-e-d by high society! For four hours I was there. My mother was saying 'You must have something to eat' but every time I tried to get a sandwich there was a white gloved hand that shook it! I don't mean the sandwich, I mean my hand!"

Is there a country in which you enjoy performing best?

"No, I like performing EVERYWHERE. It's very necessary that I do this. Another purpose of my work is to bring down all boundaries between countries. To me, it's all one space which we must share. I'm happier away from England because I don't find so much aggression on the streets elsewhere. Latin people are much more honest. That's what I hate about the English — It's their dishonesty.

The critics here accuse me of being pretentious. I look at the English and I see so much beauty there, as beautiful as the fields and the tradition they've destroyed. They're even destroying themselves with this superficial normalness, this safeness.

Never at any time of my career have I made any compromises. My work and also what David Bowie's work has endeavoured to do is just to encourage people to be themselves and, perhaps, to be a better self as well....

We rise and leave to take some photographs. Kemp is excitable, eager. He tries to avoid his manager as he considers the park (some distance away) to be a suitable place to take pictures. The manager catches sight of him and Kemp runs, laughing like some tiny, delicate child denied the opportunity to dance....　●

David Currie

Natasha Kornilof – From Pierrots to Matadors

Somewhere in South London, not too far from the river, hides a hectic basement workroom, brimming with fabrics of every description, patterns, threads, buttons, braids and new designs. A room in a state of elegant panic.

The basement belongs to Natasha Kornilof, a lovely lady who has helped dress a thousand stars and television shows, ballet companies, theatre productions and, course, one particular person who changes characters almost as often as Natasha changes threads, Mr. Bowie.

Their first encounter came in the summer of 1967, after Lindsay Kemp had informed her of 'a rather curious young man, a little stiff but with a lovely voice'. They met soon after and have remained in touch, on and off, ever since.

Natasha is one of the most respected theatre designers and costume makers in the business, her general work-load and modesty cannot hide that fact. A normal turnover for her any time is six productions, mostly consisting of TV work for dance orientated shows.

Her involvement with David Bowie has yielded some of his most famous visual images. From clowns to tours and back again....

We should really start at the beginning, so how did you come about such a lovely name?

"Because I am Russian on my father's side and I think my mother had finishing reading 'War and Peace' just before I was born — so that's why I was christened Natasha.

The luckiest thing that ever happened to me is that I was born in England, that was my personal silver spoon. My father met my mother in India and they married there. I was born in England while they were on holiday and we all returned to India when I was about three months old. We had one more trip to England when I was four, then it was back to India until fourteen when we moved to Africa. I hated Africa.

When I was 21, I came into some money from my father's estate which I used to come over here and put myself through art college.

My mother wanted me to do a 'nice course in commercial art', I think she meant graphics. I went to enrol at the Regent Street Poly — now closed — knowing nothing about art colleges or how the courses were run and here on the enrolment form was a choice of things labelled 'craft', and because I had been doing some designing with an amateur operatic society in Africa, I put an X next to theatrical design, that sealed my fate.

I did two years at the Poly and another three years in the theatre department of the Central School of Arts and Crafts and graduated with a certificate and very high hopes. Off I went with three other students saying 'We are going to open a costume business which will be bigger than Bermans' and do you know, nobody stopped us. Of course, as we knew nothing about costume businesses, things soon started to go wrong and one by one we dropped out until I was eventually left on my own in dismal premises in Berwick Street. Around this time I began doing quite a lot of work for the Oxford Playhouse. I used to design about every third show for them and make the costumes for the other shows. On a production of Volpone which was brought to town and financed by **Sean Connery** — who also dined the whole company wonderfully at the Garrick club — I met **Lindsay Kemp**. Amazing Lindsay. He was playing a dwarf in Volpone — did the whole thing with his knees bent under a bigged hooped robe. We used to travel up and down to Oxford on the train for rehearsals and fittings and Lindsay began to tell me about plans and projects for shows. When Lindsay spoke it was like an explosion of inspiration. I began to see costumes and sets in my head. I couldn't wait to work with him and then he told me he wanted me to meet this wonderful young singer, very strange, very curious voice — you must hear him.

And so, David was brought and he sang these beautiful little songs about coats and little tin soldiers. They were lovely songs."

Did you hear them from the LP?

"I heard them all from David, he sang them in the show. We listened to the LP, too."

Which show are we talking about?

"Pierrot in Turquoise". We hired a battered transit van off 'Nick the Maltese' and went off on an unlikely tour here and there. I was

♦ "David throws out ideas better than most people. He has a lovely succinct turn of phrase."

designer/driver. Of course it wasn't a financial success because nothing that Lindsay did ever was, and it became essential that we all went off and earned some money on our own account. Lindsay, Jack (Birkett) and David did some funny mime on television as I remember, and I had to accept an offer from the Dance Centre to open a costume business. That is another story, very hard work and all a bit of a nightmare. After three years I left taking most of the customers with me. From there on I was freelance again which must be about 1969 and I've been freelance ever since."

When you design, what kind of idea do you need from a customer for the best results?

"If someone like David or Lindsay ask me, they know that they only need throw out the hint of an idea to motivate me and the result will be quite astounding. Costumes emerge from me like sculpture, it's my own way of expressing myself like a painter or writer. David throws out ideas better than most because he had a lovely succinct turn of phrase, which is why he writes such good songs. He says it very simply. When he wanted the clown costume *(for the 'Ashes to Ashes' video)* he rang, we hadn't spoken for something like two years, but it was instant — it was there. He said 'You know the beautiful clown in the circus? Well, I want to be the most beautiful'. I said 'All right, what colour?' and he said 'Blue' and that was it. He didn't demand to see drawings or have copious fittings. I turned up with it just about finished and we had to make a small alteration to the neckline. Then he said he would like a hat and that was all — it was as simple as that. *(Making a clown costume like that is simple?)* The customer only needs to say the right words and David says them."

After 'Pierrot' what was the next thing you worked on with David?

"David brought Angie to meet me. At that time he wanted a costume which he called 'A cross between a Matador and a Matelot' which I thought was quite sweet. I did something for him which he wore but it was not totally successful — the style was right but the fabrics were wrong.

Then came the show at the Rainbow *(August 1972)*. I remember it well. The idea for it stemmed from something I had done for 'Pierrot' when I had crocheted a gold elastic body suit for Lindsay. This time I crocheted in fine white elastic — ten of them — crocheting in elastic very fast makes for very hot hands indeed!

I also made a copy of the little Japanese leather costume he used to wear *(as Ziggy Stardust)*, the one with the little animal designs on it. The original had begun to split, so I made a copy of it in ciré jersey and painted it exactly like the original."

I suppose the next thing you were involved in was the 1978 tour?

"I was booked to fly to Berlin for a couple of days for a meeting with David when my sister, who usually lives in Portugal, arrived to stay. She was in the middle of a nervous breakdown and the night before I was due to go to Berlin she took it upon herself to tell me all her troubles. We sat up in this room sharing her problems over a bottle of Portuguese brandy, of which, beware. It was late and I had a plane to catch in the morning. I got to the top of the stairs when the brandy hit me like a crowbar and I actually fell all the way down the stairs. I was so ill with that brandy. I got up in the morning feeling like death. I had forgotten to book a cab the previous night. There was a dense fog over London, a petrol strike and hardly any petrol in the car. I drove to Heathrow — who knows how, I don't. I checked in for my flight only to be told they had just closed the books but not to worry because there was another flight in two hours time. After that, all the planes were delayed by the fog and the lounge at Heathrow became a real tip.

Well, we eventually took off and what they had failed to tell me was that the flight was to Frankfurt! I arrived in Berlin in the dead of night and freezing cold. Coco met me with a taxi and we drove over to the film location of 'Just a Gigolo'. In that taxi I discovered that Coco and I had attended, at different times, the same convent school in Kashmir!

After David had finished filming, we went to my hotel and had about one hour to discuss the clothes for the '78 tour. We both did drawings on the back of envelopes and said 'Right, I'll go away and make the stuff'. That was about all the consultation we had."

How did the actual shape of the baggy trousers come about?

"Well, I'll tell you — We had scribbled on our envelopes and torn out bits of magazines and had lots of ideas and we knew we wanted trousers that were kind of BIG and we also wanted to combine them with Hawaiian jackets, you know, those funny shirts that men used to wear in the '40's, the ones with strange prints on them. But we had also seen a funny double-breasted mess jacket in another photograph and I wanted to combine the mess jacket with the large trousers."

Was that the snakeskin thing?

"No, that was for something else I had in mind. In fact, I wanted the snakeskin jacket to go over a series of velour track suits. I mean, you say tracksuit now and everyone is out jogging, but at the time it was something different and the velour was a new material — corduroy suits, a dark green and a brown

suit with big shoulders in ciré which was very difficult to tailor. Then David was briefly in London and I sent some stuff over for him to try on and he said 'More of this and more of that'. I didn't even see him that time, I just went away and made some more. Then he asked me if I would go to Dallas. So I got on a plane with two huge suitcases full of mountains of stuff — all these Hawaiian jackets in funny Japanese prints and off I went to Dallas. I didn't know where I had to go or who would meet me — I was just told to wait at the airport. I kicked my suitcases into the arrival lounge and there I was, jetlagged, unclaimed and £50 in dollars on me and that was it. I decided to make friends with the Tannoy announcer so every 15 minutes he put out this unlikely message 'Will the person who has come to meet Natasha Kornilof pick her up in Claim Area C'. It was two hours later and I started to get worried. One of the roadies, Loopy Ron was my name for him, had already been to the airport before the plane had landed, turned around and gone straight back to Coco saying 'I'll lay my job on the line that she isn't on that plane'. Coco couldn't believe another travel arrangement up the spout. She phoned my home. They had waved goodbye to me the previous day. Finally, Coco called the airport and they said, 'Oh yes, we have her here'. So Loopy Ron was despatched

♦ *Ziggy showing off the copy costume. Circa 1973.*

again and did a better job of it this time. David didn't want to look at any clothes that night and suggested that I go straight to bed. I was in such a state that I was incapable of sleep so I went out with the entire company and we were entertained at a French restaurant. They all ordered snails, I didn't and they were all ill afterwards including David. I eventually got to bed around 3am only to wake up three hours later in a state of

Another costume idea for Kemp's 'Salome'.

Ralph Hulett

◆ *On tour 1978, wearing his most popular combination from the large wardrobe prepared by Natasha.*

hyperactivity. I wanted to iron all these clothes that David had never seen. They told me to go back to bed. I think they thought I was raving mad. David surfaced around 11am and we had a grand try-on of absolutely all the clothes. His initial idea had been that I would prepare this large wardrobe and that he would wear one or two different combinations for each concert. In fact, when it came to it, his favourite combination was the white trousers with the snakeskin jacket. The shock of my life came when I saw the show at Earls Court and I was surrounded by people in bad copies of my trousers. The cut of the trousers was based on Jacobean breeches but I made them in white drill and down to the ankles.

David is absolutely the perfect clothes horse. You can just hang your creations on him and there they are — superb! There are very few people you can do that with. Lindsay is one of them. I know that he is little and rotund but you could put him in a flour sack

and he would make the most of it. People like him and David are always a pleasure to dress."

Did you like the show itself?

"Yes, I loved it. Particularly 'Fame' and its wonderful lighting effect. I also loved David singing the **Kurt Weill** song. In fact, I wish he would do an evening of Kurt Weill, I think his voice is so right for the songs."

Did you see the opening show?

"Yes, I travelled to San Diego. There were still things to get together, more shoes, red ones, a yellow flower as a buttonhole for the finale suit. I also did some alterations on a hired sewing machine in my hotel room. Then the show opened at a huge stadium and I was backstage for that and it was quite something."

Something I wanted to ask you earlier. Is it true that you and David painted the back-drop for the stage for 'Pierrot in Turquoise'?

"Yes. I designed it to look like a Victorian poster and we used it like a safety curtain. It had on it everyone in their costumes. Lindsay, Jack and David plus a little dog in a ruff. It had the show's title written in gold around the top. I've lost the drawing I had of it and God knows who has the cloth. It was a front cloth, not a back-drop, and I had to rig a system of pulleys, operated by David, to fold it out of the way."

I believe Lindsay had it last and when I asked him about it he said it had been

RCA

◆ *"It's quite amazing to know that after all the years David hasn't changed."*

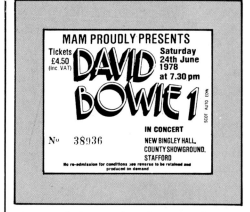

impounded somewhere because of money problems ....

"Yes, that does sound like Lindsay. David helped me lay in the background of the cloth on the floor of my attic flat in Greenwich. It was a lot of hard work and when it was over we watched 'The Magical Mystery Tour' on my TV which was on the blink. That was Boxing Day 1967. As we watched the film the picture was gradually shrinking in front of our eyes and eventually went down to a 2″ circle."

When you did that show, Lindsay was always saying that David was always saying that he always needed attention. As you were actually driving them around that was the case?

"Well, I'll tell you something about David. He's not an acquisitive person at all. He doesn't care for possessions very much. He's always either hungry, or tired, or cold, or any combination of the three, and if you can satisfy his immediate demands, like put another coat on him or feed him something, of which he will eat only a bit, or make him a little nest to sleep in, he's absolutely and totally happy. Then he wakes up and goes to work.

It's quite amazing and lovely to know after all this time he hasn't changed, he's just the same. When we were in Dallas he became instantly hungry after the trying on session and Coco had to put on something together for him to eat. She's marvellous at that, she can cook a meal over a candle. She is a lovely person anyway. It's a tough old job and she is perfect at it. We get on very well. There have been so many odds and ends I have done for David over the years I tend to forget exactly what I have done. A funny air hostess costume, all in blue, I did for his appearance on 'Saturday Night Live' in the States. He can call me anytime and I'll always consider it a pleasure to help him..." ●

[signature: John Hutchinson]

John Hutchinson — Buzzing with Feathers

The Buzz, Feathers, The Spiders from Mars: Mod, Mixed-media and the inter-galactic. Names and descriptions of three very varied bands created and nurtured by David Bowie, but linked in this case by John Hutchinson.

John 'Hutch' Hutchinson is a likeable and accomplished guitarist, singer and songwriter from Scarborough, someone Bowie depended on as a collaborator in his early days of songwriting and performing. That friendship and dependence is highlighted in **Ken Pitt**'s book, which features notes written by David. They refer to LP ideas by 'David Bowie and Hutch', and in another paragraph of the same letter he also wrote, 'Hutch should be back with us during next week so then we can really start the club zapping month.'

John Hutchinson is a typical hard working Yorkshireman. Still youthful and energetic in appearance, he is little changed from his days in the late 60's with Feathers — though not quite fresh-faced enough to want to wear the mod hairstyle he sported with The Buzz! Hutch was known to nestle on the borders of success with early Bowie ventures, from the Bowie Showboat to an involvement with the preparation of 'Space Oddity' and 'Love You Till Tuesday', through to the rewards brought with the 'Aladdin Sane' world tour of 1973. Until that time, major success seemed to elude him.

Mick Rock

THIS PARTICULAR story starts in February 1966 and John Hutchinson takes the lead....

"I was in London hoping to get a boat back to Sweden after working a year there, having first got a work permit cleared, but the work permit was never cleared. So, I hung about for a week or two and just happened to find Wardour Street and the Marquee Club. There was only one guy there, who turned out later to be **Jack Barry.** I started talking to him and I told him I was keen to find a band in London if there was one, and he said he did know somebody who was auditioning the following week and gave me the phone number. When I called, David answered and told me to come on the Saturday. There were all kinds of guitarists and drummers already there and as far as I can remember I just got up on stage on my own. David asked me to play a **Bo Diddley** beat, just sussing out if I could play. I don't remember actually running through with the band."

So the Buzz didn't exist then?

"No, The Buzz started with me, really because **Spike Palmer** — who was Bowie's roadie then and had previously worked for the Stones — said, 'David wants you in. He's going to ask this other band if they will play with him but Hutch will have to be in the band as well.' But they didn't fancy that idea, obviously, because they had their own guitarist. So he picked a bass player and

drummer that he had already seen and I brought down **Derek Boyes,** — 'Chow'. He wasn't on the phone so I telegrammed him and asked him if he would come down to London and join us, and he did.

So The Buzz really started with me. The other guys weren't at the audition, or if they were I didn't see them, but they had already seen Dek and Johnny Eager. Not long after I met them all at **Ralph Horton's** flat, which was where we used to rehearse. We would be doing 'London Boys' and those kind of things and all four of us were really quite impressed. Chow was very much like me, into R&B, and we found that we could put the same kind of 'chops' that we used for R&B into those early songs. We played them completely differently from the 'Lower Third' way of playing, from what I've gathered and heard. They seemed quite happy with the way it came out anyway."

Did you get to know Ralph Horton very well then, or did he dip out very early on?

"No, I left when Ralph was still there, so I didn't really know what had happened after I left until I saw Chow several months later when the whole thing had packed up. I never got on particularly well with Ralph although we didn't have any fights or anything, but I didn't reckon much to him myself."

Do you remember your first gig with the Buzz?

"It might have been the Marquee... I know one of the first ones was at the Marquee and somebody came up with the idea of 'The Bowie Showboat' which was a Sunday afternoon thing. I think we may have played a couple of evenings before that but I think the Marquee would have been the first gig."

What other venues were you playing in then?

"I can remember an abortive tour of Scotland. We went up to do a week or a ten day tour and ended up playing only about four gigs. I remember walking about, in Edinburgh because that one was cancelled. We played Glasgow, Green's Playhouse as it was then, with **Johnny Kidd and the Pirates.** I can remember playing California Ballroom, Dunstable the night before I got married in London and David tried to talk me out of it! He didn't come to the wedding."

Were you on the radio broadcast that featured the performance of 'Over the Wall We Go'?

"No, I didn't do any radio with them, that would have been **Billy Gray** I suppose.

(Sadly, Billy Gray died in 1984) I never met him you know and I didn't know anything about him until I read Ken Pitt's book. Those radio shows were also made at the Marquee. It was a good gig, the Marquee club. We played with other bands like the **Spencer Davis Group.** I remember **John Baldry** used to come in to watch Bowie, and **Elton John** was playing piano in Long John Baldry's band – but he was a little chubby piano player. I didn't pay much attention to him at the time. We did actually play with **Bluesology** once."

Who was Bowie spending his time with then?

"As far as I can remember he would just be at Ralph's flat, buzzing about, seeing people with Ralph on business. I didn't meet many other friends of his."

Did you know he was friendly with people like Pete Townshend?

"Yeah, we used to be walking down the street and I remember bumping into **Roger Daltrey** and one of the Kinks, **Ray Davies** I think. I believe we met **Marc Bolan** in the street but I can't remember whether that was then or whether it was when I was in Feathers with him. So we'd bump into people like that but I never socialised with them really."

Did you ever meet Ken Pitt early on?

"I think Ken Pitt was starting to be around and I might have met him during those Buzz days, but it might have been only once or twice. It could be that I didn't meet him, but I heard about him. I knew that there was this other guy with a bit more going for him than Ralph that was in the background somewhere. Maybe I didn't meet him actually because I do remember when I got together with David the second time in Feathers going to meet Ken and it was 'Pleased to meet you, heard a lot about you', that type of thing."

So how many shows do you think you did with The Buzz?

"Oh, quite a lot. I would say that I was in The Buzz longer than Billy Gray was. The Buzz was starting to break up when I left it, Billy Gray was drafted in for the recording and stuff like that. The three of them, when I left, decided to carry on by themselves and do gigs as a three piece. It started to go down hill pretty badly before I left, there wasn't a lot of gigs to do then."

Why was it going down?

"There wasn't that many gigs, we weren't getting out on to the London circuit apart from the Bowie Showboat. A lot of the other bands were getting out into the provinces, we weren't, not enough anyway. We should have been playing three or four times a week but we would probably only do just one."

During the Bowie Showboat, do you remember his mother coming down?

"No, I don't remember that. But I did meet them quite a few times when I visited David at his home in Bromley."

So why did you actually leave the band?

"I was a bit tired of being skint, and it looked like it was Ralph's fault. Certainly not any lack of ability on the band's part, we always went down well wherever we were playing. I suppose I lost confidence in Ralph and I got a bit sick of not having any money because I had a wife to look after."

So, it was an amicable break?

"From my side it might have been, apart from me and Ralph, because I suspected that Ralph was fairly happy that I went because I was the one that complained about the bread. There certainly wasn't any bust-up, there was no falling out."

Did you keep in touch with the band?

"I didn't really. I probably kept in touch with Chow but not with Dek and Ego and not really with David either. I didn't look him up until I came back from Canada. I was there for six or seven months."

How did you find David when you came back?

"I think I wrote to him at his parents' address in Bromley. I've always been loose with addresses but I must have got in touch there. Later on I got in touch with him through **John Cambridge**."

So, this leads us to Feathers. You got back in touch with Bowie, what happened then?

"I went round to see him at Clairville Grove where he lived with **Hermione**."

Did you eventually move in?

"I didn't, no. I might have stayed there one night, but that was all. I was around there a lot, but I was living with Denise and Christian in Finchley and then in West Hampstead. I worked as a draftsman and most evenings would go to Clairville Grove and take part in the creative process; like co-writing 'Space Oddity' — only joking David!"

Did you actually do that at Clairville Grove?

"Yes. All I would do was go along and sit in with David and put in bits of ideas for songs."

Weren't you instrumental in putting 'Space Oddity' together with David?

"I suppose the way it was conceived and put together was all in David's head, as everything was really. But he would always have another musician or musicians to feed off his original idea and contribute."

Was it around then that you found out that he was putting a film together, 'Love You Till Tuesday'?

"Yes. I think that had started to be planned before I was on the scene. But David was quite keen that I was in it. 'Space Oddity' was recorded specifically for that, in Denmark Street Studios I think. I can remember a couple of sessions anyway."

Ken Pitt has the original demo of that track, I wonder if you were on that or only on the version which appeared in the film?

"I don't really know. We did have a Revox around at Clairville Grove, so we might have. Certainly I would have been on the original I think."

Didn't you write some of the chord arrangements?

"I think he probably showed me one as well. He showed me something that one of the guitarists in The Lower Third did, and I think we incorporated that. I might have put the minor seventh in. He knew what he wanted but he probably didn't know how to play it or what it was called.

Again, I didn't socialise too much with him because I had the family with me. I would still go down Wardour Street a lot, we would go in The Ship if there was nothing else to do. I remember meeting **Pretty Things** and people like that."

When they were filming did you go down to the whole filming or just the bits you were involved with?

"Just the bits I was involved with really. I knew that he was doing 'the Mask' but I didn't know about the other things."

What about 'Space Oddity', you must have known that something was being done with that?

"No, not really. We were looking for a record deal, which would have been 'David Bowie and Hutch', but that was when I left. I was sitting at my drawing board in Scarborough and I heard it on the radio and realised that it had been released and David — sometimes he got them finished, sometimes he got lyrics and we'd put chords together and that."

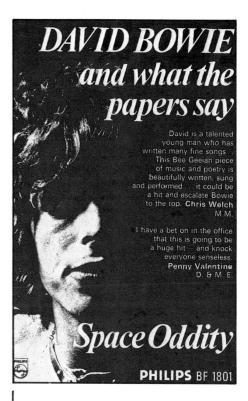

So when you recorded it in Denmark Street, that was the last you heard of it?

"Yes, until it first started getting played and then it was a hit for the first time. I didn't even see a finished version of the filming, I didn't see any of the film at all. The first time was when Ken sent me a copy of the video."

When you were filming were you aware that David and Hermione were breaking up?

"I think I was. I knew about her leaving to be in another film — whether she was going out with one of the actors was a possibility. I didn't get involved with any arguments or anything but I did realise they were splitting up. David and I went on with Feathers as a duo for a while of course."

Do you remember any of the strange shows you did with Feathers?

"Yes, Drury Lane I remember. The Arts Centre downstairs, we passed the hat around. We had a tape recorder and my job was to switch it on for the mime pieces. 'The Mask' he did alone and a couple of others he did with Hermione who danced, of course. But during the mime pieces I used to play guitar along with the tape, make *avant garde* guitar noises. I used to scrape strings and tap the guitar and things like that. I also had to learn some bits of poetry. I remember David did 'Love On A Bus' and I did a couple of real short ones because I was quite embarrassed having to read poems out, sitting on a stool. It was all a bit arty for me. So we did that; poetry, dance, mime and that preceded some other multi-media things which happened later. So David was doing that in advance of others really."

Do you remember the time when David was wearing a silly wig which he wore after having most of his hair cut off to appear in 'Virgin Soldiers'?

"Yes, I do. I also remember in 'Love You Till Tuesday' a wig he wore for that which was just a piece around the back to cover the ears because his hair was still growing back." *(If you look closely at the video of LYTT you can see the hair-piece by the shading of the hair).*

So after the last Feathers show, performed as a duo with David, you left again?

"Yes. Again because there wasn't much happening and I was sick of getting skint again. I never liked living in London particularly, but of course I liked working there... I felt that it was time to leave but I must have timed it quite badly for 'Space Oddity'. The way it turned out though, David disappeared again for a while, so there wasn't any real back-up for that song anyway."

The next thing then would be the 1973 tour, how did that come about?

"I read about Bowie increasing the size of his band in an article in the Melody Maker. He mentioned that he was going to add two sax players and he was also going to get a guy to play twelve string so that he didn't have to play it on stage. So I thought that was the job for me, if he hadn't already got somebody. I got in touch with John Cambridge who gave me David's Haddon Hall address and I wrote to him there. **Mick Ronson** phoned me at work and said, 'David wants to speak to you' and he said. 'If you can go with us we leave for New York next week.' There wasn't any audition or anything, they just offered it on the phone. I took the day off work the next day and went down to see them and they were just finishing off 'Aladdin Sane' in the studio, so I didn't play on that."

Would that have been at Trident again?

"Yes. It was strange because that was more or less where I last left him when we were recording things like 'Ching-a-Ling'. Then it was straight off to New York where I met **DeFries** and the rest of the band and we rehearsed at RCA Studios in a huge room that felt like a cinema. It had a huge screen which they used to record sound tracks. **Harry Belafonte** was upstairs and he came down to

ask us to keep the noise down. He was very nice about it all, though.

We went to New York and spent about a week there and then started rehearsing for the first show, which was Radio City Music Hall. During that time I did socialise a lot with David, we went to see **Charlie Mingus** at the Village Gate and things like that. As the tour went on we kind of lost touch as things got more complex generally. There was a lot of pressure on David all round then because the second American tour and Europe was being talked about, and as those things presumably started to fall apart he decided to pack it up, he didn't see very much of anybody. Radio City was magic, a hell of a first gig."

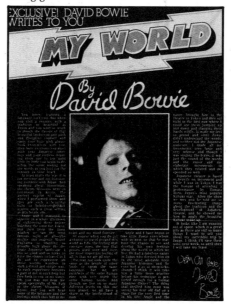
EXCLUSIVE! DAVID BOWIE WRITES TO YOU — MY WORLD By David Bowie

So within a matter of days from reading an article in Melody Maker and calling Bowie, you were in New York?

"Yes, within about ten days. I had been prepared for the audience reaction because I'd spent a few days with Mick and Trevor at their flat in Beckenham. They said, 'You're not going to believe it' because they had toured before and had a good reaction and they were dying to get back on the road again. It was reasonably easy for me because I was only standing at the back reading chords, playing rhythm. I was enjoying it really, doing my little bit and just watching as I didn't have a huge responsibility."

You were obviously meeting some weird American people at the time...

"Yes I was, especially the Mainman crowd; **Tony Zannetta, Leee Black Childers, Cherry Vanilla and Jamie Andrews.** I remember I met all kinds of people like **Todd**

Rundgren, Alan Ginsberg, and the **New York Dolls** I met at Max's Kansas City."

Because this was still early days for Bowie in America, wasn't he still running about with Lou Reed and **Iggy Pop?**

"Well, Iggy Pop was around and I may have met him in New York. I do remember he was asleep up on the roof of the hotel in Los Angeles. I went up to the roof one afternoon and he was flaked out at the top of the stairs and I had to step over him. We were supposed to be in New York in secret for the first week while we were rehearsing for the tour, but the word soon got around so there was plenty of attendance at the hotel after a few days."

Did you find life on the road hard work at all?

"No, not at all. It was all very well organised, well planned. We were picked up and dropped off in limousines, flew everywhere apart from New York to Philadelphia when we went in a bus. If we hadn't drunk into the early hours of the morning and generally done the rock 'n' roll thing, it wouldn't have been hard at all. We would stay up all night and generally get wrecked! We did a fairly strenuous tour of England and Scotland later of course. That got a bit harder."

After America you went on to Japan didn't you?

"Well, we came back from Los Angeles to England and I went home to Scarborough for a few days. A few days after that we went off to Japan to prepare for the shows out there."

Were the receptions in Japan a continuation of what you had seen already?

"Yes, it was, but the venues were smaller and the business approach was much different. The Japanese are completely different to the Americans. It was all much more sedate until the actual gigs started and there wasn't much wild goings on even after the gig was over. We were in quite posh hotels and we were obviously expected to behave ourselves. Whereas in America, everyone was crashing about being rock 'n' roll stars, in Japan it wasn't as accepted.

Who else was out there with you?

"**De Fries** was there, **Angie** and **Zowie.** We travelled everywhere by Bullet train and I remember playing with Zowie on the train and chatting with Angie."

I remember you telling me once about a rehearsal that was attended by Paul and Linda McCartney...

Ray Stevenson

♦ *Feathers, sans Hutch (Left to right: John Hill, Hermione Farthingale, D.B.).*

"Yes, that was after Japan and before the British tour. We were rehearsing for that in a cinema in London which I think was owned by **Led Zeppelin.** While we were rehearsing, Paul and Linda McCartney arrived and stood at the back listening for a while and then came over to the stage to talk. Linda spent most of the time talking to David and I remember having a natter with Paul about this and that. That was quite interesting."

Considering that you are one of those rare people who have known Bowie over such a wide and varied period of time, did he seem to change much to you?

"He didn't seem any different at first, but having been on three different tours in a row... If I said that I needed anything somebody would take me in a car to get it. Bowie wouldn't have to get out of bed. He was spoilt to death by his entourage, small though it was. But he was living that life. He was always OK to me quite honestly. The last time I saw him was on the dance floor of the Café Royal after the last gig. We exchanged a couple of words, it was all matey stuff but he knew I was leaving. That was the last time I

spoke to him. I did actually phone afterwards to leave my number and I spoke to De Fries who said, 'David can't speak to you right now, he's a bit busy. I'll pass your message on,' and that was it. He did actually say something on the radio once when someone asked him about me, something like 'I don't know what happened to Hutch'."

When you did get back together in '73, did you reminisce about the old days?

"Yes we did. He was very much like he used to be. He sort of said, 'Didn't think we would ever get to this did we', that sort of thing. I can also remember him asking me some words for some songs. He used to do an acoustic thing in the middle of the set, when he would sit on the stage with a 12-string. In fact he would use the guitar that I had for it. He would take the guitar and say, 'Do you remember the second verse to this one,' that type of thing."

If you were see David Bowie today, is there anything you would like to say to him?

"No, not really. I would more or less like to know if he's happy and together because it's

hard to tell. You see interviews on the TV and in papers and so on, and I know the way they build stars up but I just hope he's happy in himself. I don't really know anything about what he does today.

As far as guitar playing goes, I'm playing better now than I ever did, and I do play as well as anybody that I hear. So maybe I would say, 'Do you fancy a guitarist for your next album?' or 'Are you touring?' So I wouldn't hold back from saying, 'How about a gig if there is one.' But only if what I did fitted in with what he wanted."

That more or less answers my last question. Would you like to play with Bowie again?

"I would, yes. Somebody as big as Bowie can get just about anybody to play with him. But I also know that he's just as likely to use somebody like me or the piano player out of Fumble because we can contribute as well as those people who have made it big in their own right. So I would be quite happy to play with him again. You never know." ●

Phil Lancaster

The Lower Third — Back To School

The early sixties saw a rash of young groups appear in every town, mostly encouraged to form by the explosive success of The Beatles. Every town had at least one group belting out dodgy rhythms from tiny valve amps at the local dance hall. Margate was certainly no different and the front-runner at the time was billed as 'South-East Kent's Best Rhythm and Blues Group' ... They were Oliver Twist and The Lower Third.

Oliver Twist and The Lower Third were a five-piece, formed from a basic nucleus of Denis Taylor and Graham Rivens. The remaining group line-up would regularly change over the years. The original group name was thought up by an early member, Graham Smith. The name itself derived from two separate connections. Oliver Twist because of the Dickens/Broadstairs connection which is just along the coast from Margate, and The Lower Third because of the youth element. Because of its length the name was eventually cropped to the more familiar Lower Third.

The early Lower Third were all Margate boys with an eye, perhaps, to just being able to make it in the music business. One of their earliest breaks was a Saturday evening gig at La Discoteque, a small music club in the lower part of Dean Street in London. There, the group would travel up from Margate in the morning, do the gig for £15 and then travel home again. The group as it was then consisted of Graham and Denis and drummer Les Mighall.

◆ *Mod — ern Love.*

♦ *The first time Bowie ever appeared on the front cover of a music paper. Had to be paid for, though!*

At first The Lower Third expected to have to play the James Brown type music that was around at the time, something Denis Taylor was none too keen on.

"Well, I was never a very good guitarist," *Denis told me,* "That type of music never appealed to me although we did start out playing it in London. We did have quite a big band together and we wanted a singer so we did auditions at the old La Discoteque club, where we used to rehearse regularly, and David came along. In fact, Davie came along with **Steve Marriott,** who went on to form The Small Faces. Davie brought along his alto-saxophone, so we didn't realise that he was a singer, and he sat in with a tenor saxophonist and they had a right old jam session. We did an old rock'n'roll number called 'Rip It Up', Marriott sang it and David played the alto-sax..."

David's arrival at the auditions wasn't unannounced, his original meeting with the group came at the legendary Gioconda coffee bar, again in Dean Street.

"I thought it was **Keith Relf** of **The Yardbirds,**" *Denis continued.* "He looked very much like Keith Relf, David must have heard that we needed a singer and when I heard that he was a singer I said 'We must have him...', he just looked so good. So I went and told him that we wanted him as our singer and he came down to the session and it went very well. Once we got together we knew he was the right fellow, he had some great ideas."

Straight away, David and his new found group got to work rehearsing, which was mostly at David's girlfriend's house in Bromley, David injecting his enthusiasm into them with his unique and still developing style. After only a few weeks, and with a repertoire of only six or seven songs, David started to hunt round for work. With the help of some hand-out literature David wrote under the title of 'Truth Shows', The Lower Third with Davie Jones gained their first live work. Their first public gig together was at the Happy Towers Ballroom in Birmingham.

David and the group would get together every day, rehearsing, playing live and occasionally to socialise.

*At the time of the audition and early rehearsals that David had with the group, the drummer was still **Les Mighall.** During a weekend when Mighall had gone home to Margate, girlfriend problems evidently got the most of him and he never returned to London. At that time the group was almost ready to gig and were left without a drummer for coming engagements.*

"I think we advertised for a drummer, I can't clearly remember," *Graham continued,* "When Phil came along he had an unusual style and looked like **Keith Moon.** His actions were a little like his but this was before Keith Moon."

At this point it seems logical to bring in Phil Lancaster, who became the drummer and fourth and final member of The Lower Third as it was then. Phil, unlike Denis and Graham, lives up in Staffordshire today but fondly remembers the days from the sixties when he was involved with David and The Lower Third.

"I was looking for a group because I was already in the business and had been knocking around for a bit and I advertised in the Melody Maker. Graham contacted me first and arranged for me to meet Dave at the Gioconda. We basically just talked as an audition, there was no actual playing involved. A couple of nights later we played together for the first time. I was pretty quick at picking up material and I didn't need to go through the material. If I remember rightly, the first gig we played was either in Brighton or somewhere more local and they arrived to pick me up in the ambulance, which they had only bought that day."

The Lower Third was incomplete without proper guidance. A short but productive life followed as a friend of the group gradually took over as manager and started to model and promote the group for bigger things. He was Ralph Horton.

Horton had originally bumped into David while in the employment of Terry King in Denmark Street. David often wandered into King's for work and a friendship with Horton was struck. Eventually, after Horton had a spell as roadie for *The Moody Blues*, David arranged an audition for Horton with the *Lower Third* at the Roebuck pub in Tottenham Court Road. Horton was impressed and became their manager. His first engagement for them was with *The Moody Blues* at the Bromel club in Bromley. At this time, Horton was sharing a basement flat with friend and business associate, Kenny Bell. That particular flat was often later to be used as a rehearsal venue for David and the group, and David spent much time there, working, writing and occasionally being photographed. The address was 79a Warwick Square, Victoria and the building still remains.

As with many of David's early ventures, his days with The Lower Third were hard and bore little financial reward. The experience, however, was a far more important commodity and was all important in creating a clear-headed attitude. The Lower Third's music and image was always good and David's early work with them certainly could not hide his real future worth.

The Lower Third had no illusions about David's talent and all felt that the collaboration of his image and front-man persona and their reliable and solid backing were sufficient enough to get them to the top.

Work for the group was always very thin on the ground and helped to eventually end the group's existence. Reality did little to damage the quality of their performance, which was always loud, professional and highly entertaining. In only a short time, the group managed to pick up a very healthy and loyal following and their London gigs were always heavily subscribed. The group worked hard to build their reputation and travelled far and wide to make a gig. A firm responsibility rested on the driver of the ambulance, Graham Rivens.

"Perhaps that's why they nick-named me 'Death', *Graham recalled.* "I used to be the driver of the ambulance, I can't remember exactly how I got the name 'Death'. I thought it was a name that was easy to remember, I wasn't a bad driver though. I was actually the

Helene Lancaster

♦ *At the Marquee '66.*

Helene Lancaster

♦ *Graham Rivens (left) pictured with Ralph Horton.*

only driver. I can remember on many occasions, I don't know who used to organise the gigs but I could have sworn at them. We would go from London to Manchester, then back for the next gig in London, then the following night up in Leeds. The rest of the group were all right, they had been sleeping all day. We used to arrive at the gigs at about 4 o'clock in the afternoon, I hadn't had any sleep because I had driven all night and then they would say, 'Come on, we've got to rehearse, that sort of thing — so I must have seemed like death warmed up!"

The ambulance referred to by Graham has, in days since, become almost as important a landmark as the group themselves. David lived the role of an up-and-coming performer, often sleeping the night in the ambulance with the group. As seems to be a tradition in rock, to be accepted as a serious contender you have to take the rough with the smooth. As a sleeping area, the ambulance was, by all accounts, quite cosy and was a gift to the group by Graham's parents.

I asked Phil Lancaster about the ambulance itself: "Before we went to France the ambulance was as we bought it. It wasn't a stretcher job, it was the type full of seats. The French trip was the first time we used it after it had been converted, which Graham and a friend did. They turned it into a much more homely place and put in a kind of bunk arrangement and it was a lot more habitable and comfortable. It was an LC ambulance, grey not white, and we used to get pulled up in it quite a bit. We used to get stopped every 200 yards in England but in France we did all right. The police used to stop us here because it had the bell and everything on it, and the 'AMBULANCE' sign on the front and side which you weren't supposed to have. It was illegal of course. Naturally we never sounded the bell but Graham used to wear a peaked cap and people did think that he was an

ambulance driver.

"Anyway, the police were always stopping us and warning us that we must take the bell off and blank out the ambulance sign but we never ever did except once. I forget where we were but a motorcycle cop stopped us and wouldn't let us drive on until we had disabled the bell and blanked off the sign, which we did and then he let us go.

"We used to have a good laugh in the ambulance, Graham used to drive us all over the country, set up and drive home. He was a bit of a wild driver but I just used to sit at the back with David, Denis used to travel up at the front with Graham and he didn't mind anything."

The actual performances of The Lower Third have also become something of an enigma, with no live recordings or films of the group ever having been made. I asked Denis, if a film of one of their gigs suddenly materialised, what we could expect to see?

"Well, we used to do what David liked.... start off with an ordinary number and work up to a crescendo. It used to be planned out quite concisely but sometimes Davie would stick in other numbers right there on the stage which I didn't really like as they were generally technically hard. The more involved ballads Davie used to do by himself on his acoustic. We were always loud and our sound did get louder as we progressed. We generally finished the set with a number from the Planet Suite — 'Mars', it was great, really loud with lots of feedback...."

Graham Rivens also remembered an odd number that they regularly featured in their set, 'Chim-Chimenee'. "We used to do that number very much in our own style!"

Of course, as with most groups, the set would change regularly as new numbers were developed and introduced and older numbers dropped. Not only that, but the type of show they were booked to do would often determine the length and style of the performance. David and the group are often remembered for the regular Saturday afternoon shows they used to perform at the Marquee. These shows pre-dated the 'Bowie Showboat' which David developed with The Buzz in the summer of '66.

The earlier afternoon Marquee bookings came via Radio London and were for sponsored broadcasts like the 'Inecto Shows' (Inecto was a brand of shampoo). It's often asked why none of these live performances have appeared on bootlegs since. Phil Lancaster provides the answer. "In actual fact,

when we played, they never put that out on the radio. We provided the music in between the acts. They would interview the hit parade artists and while they were setting up for that, we would entertain the audience with short sets. One week **Stevie Wonder** was on and they interviewed him and played his record, that was taped and then we went on and did a set. They may have taped it but it was never taped for broadcast. I can't remember any of our gigs being taped, if they were it was without me knowing."

Rare tape collectors fear not though. Phil does recall something they did for Radio Luxembourg. "Something which I do remember being recorded was a Luxembourg show with **Shaw Taylor**(!). He used to be on the pop scene, which does seem rather hard to imagine now I know. **Muriel Young** was the producer, and we were featured on that. It was for our first record, 'You've Got A Habit Of Leaving Me'. I remember we worked out a little dance routine for that at Ralph's flat, they played the record and the studio was full of kids. We danced along with it and then **Shaw Taylor** interviewed David. I remember listening to that when they broadcast it, so I know that was taped. The only other recording we made, other than records themselves, was for the BBC. It was an audition tape for them, whatever happened to that I don't know."

It musn't be forgotten that David and the group also recorded a number of commercials for US radio. One was by Denis' brother-in-law and was a tune called 'It's a Lie' — re-written by David for a product called 'Puritan' — whatever that was. Another was for Youthquake Clothes.

Although there is no live performance film footage of DB and the lads, it can be revealed that there is some 8mm film, taken on the Isle of Wight ferry trip in '66 by Ralph Horton, and also of the group messing about on the seafront at Bournemouth — but we defy you to find that on any video list!

*In all David and The Lower Third released two singles, 'You've Got A Habit Of Leaving'/'Baby Loves That Way', which was produced by **Shel Talmy** and 'Can't Help Thinking About Me'/'And I Say To Myself', produced by **Tony Hatch**. David wrote the songs but the group as a whole naturally took a lot of private credit for the overall finished sound. As all the group informed me, the songs were very much a joint effort.*

David naturally encouraged total

102

♦ *Pictured at Ralph Horton's flat, 1966.*

Pictorial Press

involvement from all of the group when it came to writing and recording new material, as Graham recalled.

"David used to sit at home and strum a guitar and write some lyrics. We then used to sit down together as a group and make the whole thing something feasible and bring the whole tune together. A lot of the early stuff we did with him, apart from the basic tune and lyrics, was very much a joint effort. 'I Can't Help Thinking About Me' comes to mind, we all did what we wanted to do and it all blended together very nicely."

Phil is also quite clear about how those early tunes came about. "David would get out a 12-string and say, 'Listen to this one' and strum through it and we would all add what we thought. This would probably be around at Ralph's and we would rehearse acoustically without amps. When we rehearsed 'live' as it were, that was usually at the Marquee or at the Roebuck — that would be with all the equipment. I can remember the songs starting off with David strumming the tune and occasionally he would introduce a new number during one of our full-blown rehearsals. A funny thing I remember about the recording of 'You Got A Habit' was that I used David's tweed jacket to hang over my bass drum to improve the sound."

Phil also remembers more recordings the group used to do on a very regular basis, which were demos for other people and groups.

♦ *Reunion '84. Left to right: Graham Rivens, Denis (T-Cup) Taylor Phil Lancaster.*

"Anything to earn a few bob then," *Phil continued.* "We really did do lots of demos, not just for ourselves and Tony Hatch, but also for groups like **The Pretty Things**. In fact one of the songs we demoed for them is featured on one of their LP's. They used it to get a better idea of the sound, then re-recorded it. Whatever happened to those things I don't know now, probably all lost."

Denis also recalled David's early songwriting. "One of the ways we would write was I would bring my fingers down on the keyboard and David would say 'What's that? Hold that chord', and he would write something around it. I found it hard getting my fingers used to those chords, he never made things easy, but they were great songs, he really was a terrific songwriter."

Over the conversations I had with the three members of The Lower Third, all three brought up their early meetings and associations with The Who. David and The Lower Third would often be featured on the same bill, but Phil remembers David's first meeting with **Pete Townshend** *and fondly recalls evenings spent with The Who.*

"We were rehearsing one afternoon for our residency in Bournemouth, and we had the stage to ourselves. The Who were also on that weekend and arrived while we were rehearsing. Pete came walking into the dance hall and we were going through Dave's stuff. Anyway, I'm convinced that they had never met before and Pete came to the stage and said, 'Whose stuff is that you're doing?' So

David replied, 'It's mine,' to which Pete replied, 'That's a bit of a cheese-off, it sounds a lot like mine!' I thought that was quite funny looking back on it now. I sat down with Pete later and we had a natter about what we were earning. He wanted to know if we were getting as much as he was. We used to bump into them quite a lot after that."

As the group's short history continued, it seemed more and more to them that money was to be the real spoiler. They were simply getting no money and the bills were ignored. Both Graham and Denis felt the pinch more, being the furthest from home. Ralph Horton was generally showing more interest in David, his young protégé and, in his view, the real star of the group. The original group idea was far more democratic which was as much David's idea as any other member. All of the group remember David being much involved in the project as a group of all of them, and the general feeling was that Ralph Horton alone began to see differently.

Denis elaborated: "We started off as a group but it soon became Davie and Ralph together and I remember that annoyed me, they used to drive off after a gig and leave us to pack up and get on with it. It was a pity, Ralph did a few things which were wrong... he even made us sign a form which wrote away all of our royalties and meant we got nothing from the records. David used to actually really muck in with the rest of us until Ralph came along. Davie even slept in the ambulance with us a few times... generally though, we drove Davie

back to Plaistow Grove."

It was also during the group's life that David changed his name. Denis remembered talking to David about it at the time.

"I remember the day quite well actually. Graham and I had been out somewhere and we went back to Ralph's flat and David proclaimed that he had changed his name. I said 'What to' and he said, 'Bowie'. I asked him why Bowie and he replied because he liked the surname of Jim Bowie, the American. At the time I didn't think 'Bowie' was a very up-and-coming star's name to pick. Many people pronounce it wrong as well, it grew into the right name though."

David's first trip abroad was a notable affair and was the highlight of the group's live work together.

"The shows themselves were arranged by our agents, Marquee Artistes", *remembered Phil.*"We were a little late arriving in Paris and the guy who had arranged to meet us was hopping up and down when we arrived but in the event we managed to get on stage on time. The actual shows went tremendously well and after we came off from each set the girls were actually belting the door down to get to us. It was an amazing reaction considering they hadn't seen or heard of us before .... that was at the Golf-Drouot club. The other gig was at the Palladium. We did about three gigs in all, two at the Golf-Drouot. **Arthur Brown** was also on the bill.

"I was the only member of the group who had played abroad before and I think it was David's first trip out of the country... he certainly hadn't played abroad before that. We had an unpaid roadie with us at the time as well.

"We were actually there on New Year's Day in '66 and were there for about three days I think. I can't remember anything out of the ordinary happening but it was a great time. I do remember something which cheesed us off a bit. Ralph arrived on the last day to pick David up and take him back ahead of us. I remember they flew back, which was David's first time on a plane. We had to struggle back in an ambulance. Ralph wanted David back earlier to meet the producer of 'Ready Steady Go!', Vicky Wickham."

Shortly after returning from France, a press party was held in London at The Gaiety Bar, Strathearn Place, Hyde Park, for David and the group's first Pye single, 'Can't Help Thinking About Me'. Invited to the reception was **Freddie Lennon,** *father of John, with* *whom David and the group posed for photos. DJ's and journalists soaked up the free drink and buffet, two days before David's nineteenth birthday.*

The high spirits of that party could not hide the fact that David and the group were gradually moving apart — not through ill feeling, but because of serious money problems that had plagued the group since its inception. The whole problem came to a head before a planned performance at Bromley's Bromel club, where David had arranged a show on behalf of his old school, Bromley Tech. When Ralph Horton again claimed that expenses were too great and that there would be no money for the group that night, the band decided to call it a day and leave. Denis continues the story:

"Ralph Horton was a bad manager, he couldn't get us enough work and in the end he was paying us no money, we just had to say 'No' to him. It was a very difficult time, I do remember that David was in tears and it was all very sad. It wasn't really fair on any of us."

Graham: "When we split up there was a bit of grievance which carried over. David was a bit annoyed because it was for his old school. It was a shame... I would like to bump into him today if those things don't worry him any more. The last time I met him was in the Sixties. I really think he's doing great things now... superb."

Phil: "It had been a sad parting for all of us, and it was all down to money. I went to the Marquee quite regularly after the group broke and I saw David with The Buzz. When he came off he couldn't be more pleased to see me and we shook hands and it was nice that it was all OK again. That was the last time we met but a funny thing happened a few years later after I had moved up here, the most strangest of coincidences. I was travelling on the boat to Sweden with my wife and we were in the lounge when I heard this familiar voice and looked to see it was Denis of all people. He was going to try and make his way in the business in Sweden and I asked him if he had seen anybody and he said he had recently seen David and that he was going for a part in 'Hair'.

"I used to hear him now and again on the radio, on some kind of Saturday afternoon show on the BBC, a kind of 'In Concert', and I used to think, 'Blimey, he's coming on'. He was really different, he seemed to know something no one else did. That gave me the feeling that some day he would do something

rather special."

Denis Taylor probably ran into David more after the group left David. For a while The Lower Third continued until they eventually split themselves and went their separate ways. Denis recalls meeting David after the split:

"Once I was coming out of the Gioconda and David was walking up the other side of the road. He called me over and said, 'Come and have a listen to this'. He had an acetate in his hand of something he had just recorded at RG Jones'. We went into a record shop cubicle and played it, it was 'Rubber Band', which I thought was a fantastic record and I told him so. We were obviously still friends and he was pleased that I liked it. The record was really good for that time but they didn't release it on time and it missed its moment.

"I also saw him once with The Buzz and I didn't like them at all, very weak and feeble in comparison with our group .

"There really is no one like David around any more, he really was a one-off. You couldn't compare him with anyone, even someone like **Boy George** won't be around in a couple of years. He's great and I hope he has

many more years success, perhaps one day we will all get together again".

Out of all the ex members of The Lower Third, the only member who has seen him in his concert since his Buzz days is Graham Rivens who travelled to see one of David's Serious Moonlight performances at Milton Keynes, Graham continued: "To be perfectly honest, his stage act had changed very little from the early days, his actual stage movements — ignoring what's going on around him of course. I thought, 'Christ! I've seen that before'. I did try to meet him afterwards but there was no chance, the security guards just looked blank, I knew they would."

Today, Graham Rivens is working in the electrical business, running his own shop near Margate. Denis Taylor has a photo agency, again in Margate. Phil Lancaster is now up in Staffordshire having moved out of London. He is working in the building material business. David Jones has remained in the music business and still occasionally brings the world to a standstill with the odd tour or two. ●

Earl Slick – Slick Conversation

Behind the pulse-pounding, screeching and soaring guitar solos that have familiarised much of David Bowie's middle 70's music, lies an interesting story.

The man responsible is Earl Slick – with a wild and characteristic mop of hair, lean frame and a decidedly rock 'n' roller face. Earl Slick has toured with Bowie twice, played guitar on two studio albums and, like Bowie himself, has endured the music business, suffered the whims of flighty managers and remained true to his ambitions – collecting experiences and discarding bad values.

In 1974 Bowie's mind was placed firmly on cracking the vast American market which had previously eluded him. He embarked on the 'Diamond Dogs' tour and through an absurdly lengthy period of gigging, nearly wrecked his mental and physical facilities. . Decadence, doom and despair made the tour a slow, painful grind which very nearly brought everything to a halt. It turned David Bowie into a 'plastic soul' singer, eventually producing songs sung with a heartfelt passion that was all but absent from his previous work.

This period was Slick's first involvement with Bowie. The next time he toured with him was in 1983 for the hugely successful Serious Moonlight shows.

Today, Earl Slick stands poised on a solo career with as much eagerness as he once had, but perhaps with a little more maturity and much more awareness of the many invisible pitfalls that chart the road to success.

▸ *Earl Slick with 'friend' in background.*

♦ The year of the ....

To describe his guitar playing as 'slick' would be an absurdly obvious comment. The player himself prefers 'aggressive' which not only applies to his musicianship but also his early commitment to become a guitarist.

Growing up in the rough area of Brooklyn known as Red Hook, Slick and his family moved around to different 'better' areas of Brooklyn and at the age of 11, they settled home in Staten Island which, as Slick remembers, "Was a nicer place to bring up a family and much safer."

The music bug bit him, as it did countless other young Americans, when four long-haired lads from Liverpool first appeared on the Ed Sullivan Show bringing with them an unequalled wave of excitement that has transcended the confines of musical history to become part of history itself.

"It was a Sunday night and we'd all heard of **The Beatles.** It was Beatles this and Beatles that, but we didn't really know what they were about. Suddenly, they appeared on **Ed Sullivan,** amidst all the usual dog-acrobatics and we all went nuts. That started me off. In school, everyone's hair was all washed down and everyone was forming bands. Nobody could play but we were all assigned different instruments. After The Beatles, Sullivan had them all on – the Stones and everyone else."

How did your parents react to all this?

"Well, at first it was like 'What is this?' because everyone was going nuts and I guess it had never happened in that way before. They were all thinking that we'd all grow out of it. But when I did convince my parents that I was serious about this, they bought me a guitar. It was the last thing my father bought for me and he said: 'OK, I'll buy you this but if you're good enough you'll find a way to buy whatever else you need.' That was good because it gave me that 'I'm gonna prove it' attitude."

There then followed a fairly typical procession of school dances and party gigs, the young Slick transporting equipment along with fellow group members on New York public transport. After gaining more stage sense, the group finally made the coffee bar and club circuits, playing for money that hardly covered their bus fare. Such was the way of many enthusiastic teenage bands, motivated by the British pop invasion and carried by the optimism of the 60's. Many did 'grow out of it', others slipped away, discouraged and forlorn. For Earl Slick, the desire remained and he continued to practise and perfect his craft through session and live work.

What could be considered to be his big break, and surely the thing which first thrust him into the attention of the rock world, was when he joined David Bowie's band touring the States in 1974:

"I had a friend called **Hank Deveto** who I grew up with. He was one of a collective group of people I knew that got out of it and started to do really professional work. He introduced me to **Michael Kamen,** who at that point just needed roadies. I'd been through the situation of trying to play your own originals around New York and usually getting thrown out because all people wanted to hear was the top 40. So, I was really disgusted. I didn't want to play any more bars, I hung around, mostly broke and decided that if I could be around the professionals, even only as a roadie, I'd be learning, making a few bucks and be much better off.

I hauled equipment for a few days for Hank's band The New York Rock Ensemble. And I used to get up on stage during sound-checks and jam with them. The band included **David Sanborn** who I was getting along with very well, especially during the jamming sessions. I think it was Sanborn who approached Kamen and said 'Why don't you let him play the gigs?', so I was hauling

equipment, then playing the gigs then hauling equipment. Eventually, Michael said I didn't have to haul gear any more and I could just play. We did about a year of gigs. In 1974 Michael had done the music for Joffrey Ballet in New York, and Bowie was in town and came to see it. David, as you know, is always going to see this or that as far as the arts go. He's always very involved. Well, he met Michael that night. This was just after he'd finished recording 'Diamond Dogs', and he told Michael that he was looking for a guitarist to go on tour with him. Apparently, they'd been auditioning all kinds of guys and couldn't find the right one.

So Michael just said 'There's this guy I've been working with, Earl Slick – he's very good' and all that. And that was how I first got involved with Bowie."

Were you aware of his work previously?

"I was, yes, but I was never a Bowie freak in any sense of the word. I liked it all, especially Ziggy, but it wasn't the same as the way I felt about The Beatles and the Stones. All I knew originally about the tour was that I would be working with guys I liked – Tony Newman, Herbie Flowers, Sanborn and Kamen of course. Kamen was putting the band together for David, so already with Sanborn and Kamen there were two people I'd already

.... Diamond Dogs.

◆ On the Dick Cavett Show, December 1974.

worked with and had a lot of respect for. I just thought 'This is amazing'."

Did you have much contact with Bowie?

"Yes, well, we used to hang around, drink a few beers and go out. He was trying to check me out and get to know me."

Did you find his theatrical ideas for the show odd after not playing in such a stage production before?

"No, not at all. It was actually very refreshing, because I was sick and tired of the music scene then. Once I got into it and met David and found out what he was all about I thought 'This is something really new and good'."

The Diamond Dogs tour, eventually discarding its elaborate sets to become the more soul-orientated 'Philly Dogs' tour, kept Earl Slick (or Eric Slick, as he was referred to in an early Melody Maker review of the shows) in employment for most of 1974, taking him to mostly East Coast areas of the States. Towards the end of its exhaustive run,

Bowie was bringing new songs into the set which he had written on the road. This material developed into the studio album 'Young Americans'. Slick was retained as one of the guitarists:

"Most of the guitar on that album is Carlos Alomar, as it wasn't really my style of playing. I did a bit here and there but it's Carlos' funk-rhythm that you mostly hear. 'Station to Station' I was much more involved with."

Does Bowie allow much freedom for solos?

"Yes. Quite often, he'd come into the studio with songs not completely written. He had the lyrics and basic tune but was missing a riff or a lick or whatever and he'd just say, 'Do what you do'. You see, David hires someone for his band because he wants whatever it is they can do. He would never ask me to do something that Carlos would do because he knows it's not natural for me to play in that style."

It's been noted that Bowie was going

through a transition period between the tour and those two albums. Was there any change you noticed?

"Something was going on. He seemed all right until the end of it, but we were all getting a little too high all the time. Everybody! The 70's was like 'Let's see how high we can get'. You look back on it now and see how silly it all was. But maybe we had to go through that to learn something. Because of it, though, I can't remember everything too well. There's huge blocks there."

Were you at the 'Young Americans' sessions when John Lennon was there?

"No. He came in on different days. We played on the same songs, but we were never in the studio at the same time. The funny thing is that when I worked with Lennon on 'Double Fantasy' he swore blind that he knew me from working on those sessions! Unless my memory is worse than I think it is we were never ever together in the studio. I don't think I'd forget that."

What was it like working with Lennon

as he was such a hero of yours?

"THAT . . . was amazing. It's still a hard one to talk about. It's very strange how it affected you. John was so easy going. I've been involved in records that I've either walked out on or been thrown off of.

Artists that don't know what they want, they have no patience and at the end of the evening they've driven you completely mad. That's why I don't do session work any more. I hate it. To just walk in coldly.

But John, just like David, wanted what you could do, gave you the room to do it and got what they wanted by not intimidating everyone around them. I mean, David and John are probably the two most major stars in the history of music. And they're both very intelligent and know that they could have an adverse effect on people just because their presence alone can make a musician nervous and nothing would happen."

Were you nervous when you first met Lennon?

"Before I got to the studio I was, but as soon as he said 'Hello' all the nerves just vanished. It was the way he was. If we were performing and it wasn't going quite right, John would break into these stories, which were usually hilarious, or make up new words, mostly unrepeatable. And we'd all be looking at each other with 'What's he saying?' looks and finally all fall about laughing being totally unable to finish the track. He'd relieve the situation with humour instead of tension."

Working with the original influence on his career, Slick counts as one of its highlights, alongside with his work with Bowie. Once, years earlier, John Lennon was just an inspiring image on the television and today Earl Slick has a memory of working with the ex-Beatle.

That was in 1980, however, and after recording 'Station to Station' Slick's career went through one of its lowlights. Due to mismanagement and bad timing, he left Bowie on less than friendly terms and declined to tour with him in 1976 – deciding instead to pursue a solo career:

"I got into this thing with David at a very young age, not all that experienced in that type of thing and there was a point when we'd just finished 'Station to Station' where we were supposed to go on the road. At the time, I'd just signed a solo deal with Capitol Records and we had this lunatic manager who was handling myself and David. I'm not going to name any names, as it's all water under the

bridge and he knows who I mean. But something was going on between him and David. David was claiming that he'd been ripping him off, this, that and the other. So they had this big falling out right at the end of the album just before the start of the tour. Now somebody else in the Bowie organisation got ahold of David and got in his ear, and then this manager got ahold of me and told me how I was going to get ripped off by David. So David and I never had another conversation about it but we were both convinced, wrongly so, that we were planning to rip each other off! The result of this was that I didn't do the tour. I didn't even show up for rehearsals which is not a very smart thing to do. Instead I went on to try and pursue a solo career knowing deep down that I wasn't ready for it. I was prematurely on my own because this manager had figured that the best way to get back at David would be to steal his guitarist out from under him. After that, I started getting really disappointed and disgusted

Larry Bulaitis

with myself. Instead of getting myself together I was getting higher all the time. And one day, I just opened my eyes to everything and said 'This is nonsense' – So that was a low point. I found myself doing session work for people I didn't want to, but it was 'I either do this or I don't pay the rent this week'. It was like a vicious circle and I slipped deeper and deeper into it until I became really disgusted with myself, saying 'Is this all you're worth?' And then I made the decision not to do any more session work for people I didn't want to. At the time, I decided that if I can't make it the way I wanted to, I'd rather sell my gear and forget the whole thing."

Needless to say, he didn't, and at the end of 1976 he formed the Overnight Angels with ex-Mott the Hoople front-man **Ian Hunter**.

Before this, he was cutting records and touring with his own group, the ill-fated Earl Slick Band, which was being handled by the same manager that had been the cause of the break-up with David Bowie, although neither Slick nor Bowie were aware of this at the time.

Eventually realising the situation, Slick abandoned his solo career and began work with Hunter. The same misfortune applied to the Overnight Angels but for different reasons:

"It was the only band I was ever in that had to break up for financial reasons rather than any internal problems", *he recalls*. "After a while it became impossible to keep the band afloat."

In 1983, Slick returned to the world of David Bowie, old problems resolved and both with a certain amount of maturity and experience that made them all the more wiser. By a strange twist of fate, the circumstances that led to Slick joining the 1983 tour band were startlingly familiar to those that had forced him to depart in 1976 – although this time around it wasn't to be him that would make the mistake.

Highly praised guitarist **Stevie Ray Vaughn**, *who provided the bluesy breaks on the 'Let's Dance' album, left the tour band under a cloud of managerial disharmony only a few days before the opening show in Brussels. His replacement was Earl Slick who only had four days to rehearse the song set:*

"I basically sat in my hotel room in Brussels for four days and nights with Carlos and went over and over it. I knew at least half the songs from previous tours or records – it was the other half that was difficult.

I hadn't seen David for about five years and I was very apprehensive about that because the way it went down when I left was not cool. But then I figured that I'd changed quite a bit and I knew that he had. You can tell where someone's at, just from reading the odd interview here and there. But even so, that was worse for me. I was more worried about that than learning the songs.

And when I met David it was like no time had passed. We were friends again."

Did the nerves hit you on opening night?

"I anticipated having a nervous breakdown before going on stage because I had two and a

s   l   i   c   k

Greg Gorman

111

s   l   i   c   k

Greg Gorman

half hours of the show in my mind getting all jumbled up. I told Carlos to keep an eye on me and cover for me if I screwed anything up. Once on stage, my nerves settled down and I was fine. Then I blew my amp during the very first song! In a way, that was good because it lifted the tension from playing and I'm glad that happened rather than me screwing up."

What was the general touring party atmosphere like this time around as opposed to '74?

"It was a lot tamer. 1974 was lunatic time. During the European leg we were all pretty relaxed but the pressure really started when we hit the States. We hardly saw David as he was being bombarded for interviews all the time."

Did you all enjoy the open air concerts?

"There are so many differences. You have to deal with Mother Nature as well as all the other things. After a while, though, I began to prefer the open air gigs, especially in the States where it was nice and warm. Milton Keynes was pleasant as well. But we also did some open air gigs in Germany which were horrendous – cold and wet. What can you do?

You've booked it, you can't just say 'We don't want to get wet, we're going home'."

How did the Far East react to you?

"Great! We really had no idea what to expect. Whether they would just sit and stare. We played Singapore, Bangkok and Hong Kong and the reaction was pretty normal, people yelling and singing and having a good time."

You played 'Imagine' in Hong Kong – When did Bowie decide to insert that?

"We were sitting on a plane, going to Bangkok, I think it was the Hong Kong gig, which was on the last date of the tour, December 8, and it dawned on me what it was. So, I went over to David and said why don't we do something as a mark of respect for John's death. I suggested 'Across the Universe' as David had covered that song with Lennon.

And David said 'Well, if we're going to do it we might as well do 'Imagine'. This was on the 4th and we rehearsed the song a couple of times in Bangkok – That's how it all happened."

The song followed 'Fame', the track from

'Young Americans' co-written by Lennon and Carlos Alomar. Bowie prefaced the performance with the following story: "I co-wrote the song with John Lennon. And I asked him 'How do you write your songs?'. He said 'It's easy, you say what you mean and put a back-beat to it'. I said 'What do you think of my rock 'n' roll?' he said 'It's great, but it's just rock 'n' roll with lipstick on'.

"The last time I saw John Lennon was in Hong Kong. We were in a market and there was a stall that sold old clothes and there was a Beatle jacket on the stall. I did something not usually in my character and I asked him to put it on so I could take a photograph. I took a photograph and I still have the photograph. The jacket doesn't fit properly. It looks like John had outgrown it. On this day, December 8, 1980, John Lennon was shot and killed outside his New York apartment...."

The Hong Kong show brought the Serious Moonlight tour to a close. The band all bade their farewells at a party in a Hong Kong club that was hired for the occasion.

Did Bowie ever comment on his feelings on the tour to you?

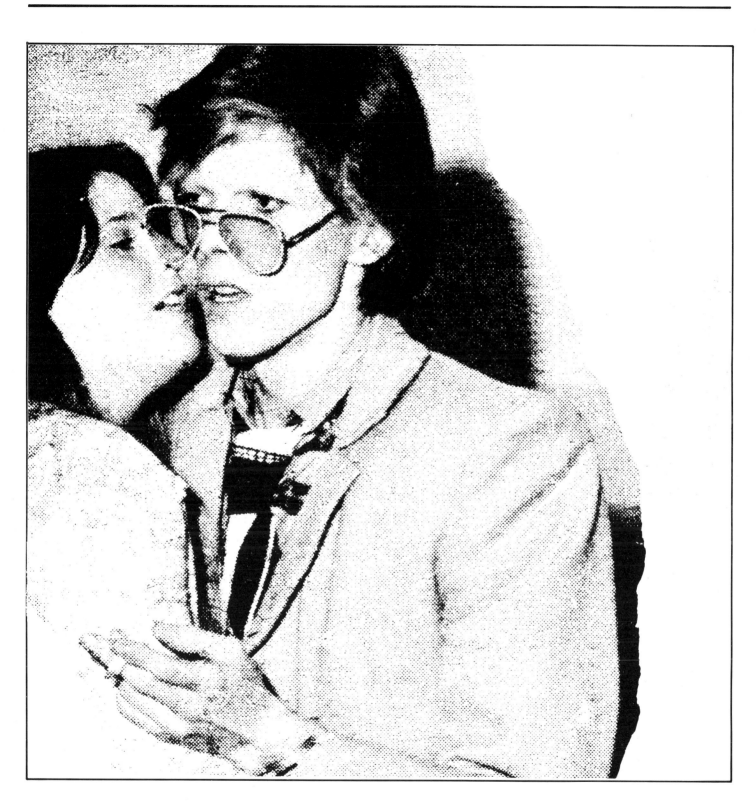

"Well, I just know one thing. You expect that he takes everything for granted, just sits back and says this is supposed to happen. But he's not like that at all. There were times when he'd just sit, bemused, and say 'This is amazing'. He was very, very pleased with the way the tour was received."

Now that the tour is just a fading memory, Earl Slick is a relaxed man, carefully looking to the future and an overdue solo career.

Whatever it is that enables a Brooklyn kid to overcome many setbacks and failures, to attract the attention of artists of the calibre of David Bowie and John Lennon, it seems that Earl Slick has it.

Perhaps the much sought-after gift of giving a guitar a vocabulary is something that is not taught or given but won through years of perseverance and tolerance. In today's music business, as in yesterday's, where proficient guitarists are a dime a dozen, it does take a little extra talent to emerge from the pack and become a successful guitarist.

Despite the barren years, Earl Slick is still there, still working for a solo career as hard as ever. Maybe this time around will be the right one. ●

Dana Gillespie – Certainly Weren't Born A Man

FACT: Dana Gillespie is alive and well and busier than ever.
FACT: David Bowie did once carry her ballet shoes after classes (not school books).
FACT: David Bowie did write 'Andy Warhol' for Dana to perform.
FACT: Dana Gillespie is still as beautiful as ever.

Dana Gillespie was born in Woking, Surrey. As well as being a contemporary of David Bowie, she is well known and documented for her own considerable writing, acting, singing and performing skills. When she was fifteen she was British water ski champion — at the same time she was also making her first inroads into the music business.

Since those days in the mid-sixties, she has spent her time earnestly building her career, regularly taking time off from writing and recording to take on stage and film roles. Performances on the British stage include roles in 'Liz', 'Catch My Soul', the part of Mary Magdalene in 'Jesus Christ Superstar', 'Mardi Gras' and 'The Tempest' for the National Theatre. Film roles have included parts in Ken Russell's 'Mahler', 'The Lost Continent' for Hammer films, 'Bad Timing', 'Slags' and most recently, a new film called 'Bones'.

I managed to steal a couple hours of Dana's time while she was on a short stay at home in London — a rare occurrence these days with the busy schedule she regularly maintains. On the morning of our conversation, time was our enemy as she was expected for a mid-day appointment at Andrew Webber's party . . . .

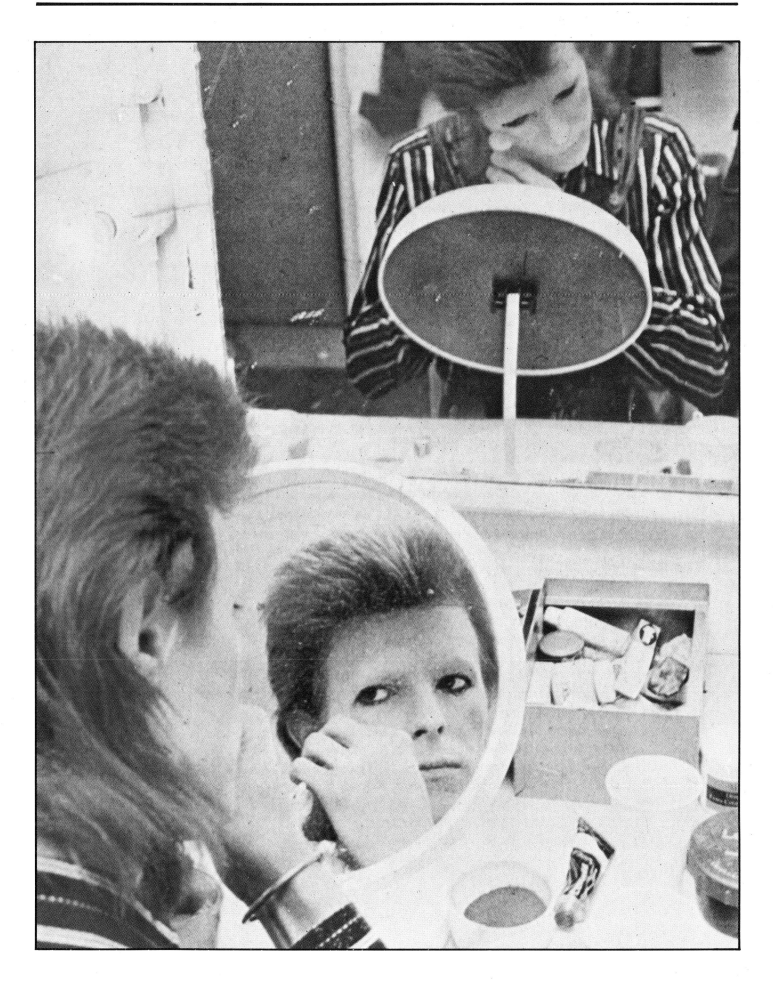

♦ *A twelve-year old David Jones in the Bromley Tech. School Class of '59 (May).*

Actually I didn't particularly like the music they did and I wasn't particularly taken with his sax playing either.

This was at the sound check, and during the break I was standing in front of the mirror at the Marquee club, brushing my hair, which was waist length and peroxided blonde. He came up from behind and took the brush out of my hand and started brushing my hair and asked me if he could walk me home that night. I said 'OK', when I saw who was at my hair, which of course was David. So we became friends then, I must have been fourteen, very nearly fifteen and he was still living at home then.

He took me home to meet his mum and dad once. We sat down and ate tuna fish sandwiches. I remember thinking, now where was this . . . . Bromley, this is the first time that I had been into a house that was built on the proportions of the sort of houses that you now see on **Coronation Street.** I had never been into one of these before, I had never seen a kitchen that was so tiny, I had never sat on chairs that had those things that catch grease on the back of them. I don't know what they're called. Suddenly, I realised that I was in somebody's home where there was a big culture difference, but that's my own personal shake-up. It didn't affect David in the end.

I remember when David would come and stay the night, I would have to sneak him up to the top floor where I lived, past my parents' bedroom. The first time he met my father, he actually thought he was a girl until the name David came up and David's hand came out and he shook my father's hand. But in those days he had hair much longer than even The Beatles did, like when they came out with 'Love Me Do', because it really was waist length and dyed bright yellow, which was very revolutionary for those days. Then I used to see him, not regularly, but sometimes he would walk me home from school. I mean, it's always romantically put in the papers that he carried my ballet shoes, well, as I went to a stage school I probably had a pair of ballet or tap shoes on me.

At this time though, I was much more concerned with writing songs and when I wasn't romping on the bed with David in the top room he'd be showing me the odd chord on the guitar. So, armed with about three chords, shown to me by David on an old Spanish guitar, I started in the music business. I was writing pathetic poetry which was an excuse for writing songs. Then one day, I was at the

"We moved to London when I was about ten and I was at a stage school from the age of thirteen having been to a very straight upper class school. While at the stage school, I moved in circles where the other children weren't of the same social class as me, and this was kind of a culture shock which I didn't realise at the time. I must have felt some form of rebellion because every night would find me down at the Crawdaddy club or Marquee club, from the age of thirteen watching the blues bands or whoever was around. Although I loved seeing the coloured blues guys, I was always very turned on to the white acts which would generally be the support acts because they were even closer to what I had imagined.

I had never even encountered black people when I was thirteen so they were a bit remote for me. So, bands like the T-Bones, and the Authentics would be playing around that era and then one night there was Davy Jones and the Manish Boys. He came on stage with knee length suede boots with fringes, a bit like Robin Hood-Sherwood Forest look, long blonde hair and a kind of loose pirate type shirt. I sat as usual in the front row with my mouth open, agog at just the musicians.

Marquee club, one of those days when I wasn't seeing David, because David would disappear for weeks on end, either being up North with his band — they used to travel around in an ambulance. He'd tell me about how they would pull birds in Piccadilly Circus because in an ambulance you couldn't see in through the windows. Anyway, Julie Driscoll would be in the audience as well, and she had become very friendly with Georgio Gomelski, who had become the one who was famous for losing the Stones, but he looked after The Yardbirds. He offered me a contract, I sang at the Marquee, pretty pathetically on my guitar.

But I looked good and in those days.... I was fifteen, big tits, had a good image, a lot of front, a lot of foolhardiness, I didn't really know what I was doing. I found myself in situations where people offered me things, so I took up the offers because there was nothing else to do. I was just working in a record store at night and delivering newspapers in the morning, and playing in the band when I had time, rehearsing.

So, during these formative years in the music business, I didn't see too much of Bowie, or David, but now I call him Bowie because everybody else does. He was busy and then I was out doing like a folk circuit with my guitar and my three chords, never imagining that I could have sung blues then, although I always loved blues. In those days there were folk clubs you could do and make fifteen quid a night, which is probably better than a lot of pubs do with rock and roll bands. I somehow managed to survive that, a few records coming out and disastrous appearances, from my point of view anyway, on **Ready Steady Go** and early mad things in the pop business. Through it all, up until 1970, I survived through making singles, I made two albums; one for Decca, 'Box of Suprises', and for London (Decca America) 'Foolish Seasons'. They had really good musicians on them like the guys from Manfred Mann or Big Jim Sullivan or Jimmy Page. The next album I did was 'Box of Suprises' and that was with Mike Vernon producing. We used one of his bands, 'Savoy Brown'. This was the first album for me which was totally my own compositions.

I would keep doing the occasional Hammer film or stage performance of some gruesome musical that wouldn't be particularly good, anything to keep busy learning my trade. Then in 1970, my years are actually very bad as to what happened when, but I always kept

friendly with David and I would see him whenever he was here, but I never saw him that much when he was with Hermione. I think I only saw him once when he played with Lindsay (Kemp) and Jack (Birkett) at the Mercury Theatre, where he played Pierrot or something like that. I remember he got me a ticket for that and I sat by myself. She was around then, but he never brought her around to my place.

I remember one time, he was living with her quite close to me in South Kensington and he came around and said, 'Listen, I've just written a song,' and he played 'Space Oddity' which he thought would do well. He also showed me his stylophone as well, which was another early thing. Up until then Rolf Harris was about the only person you ever saw with a stylophone. He also came round to me in tears when he and Hermione had split up. I didn't see him so much in that era until he met Angie and when I met Angie she and I got on very well, I had a boyfriend then who was a writer.

The four of us used to hang about together.... this must have been around 1972. Anyway, we just kept friends and I just kept pissing about.

I went to the States for a short while and when I got home, David said to me, 'I've met this guy who I think is a really good agent/manager, you should meet him'. So that's how I met De Fries. I was taken up to the office in Regent Street and there was this guy with a ton of woolly hair on his head, looking like a Jewish afro. I got on very well with De Fries, I instantly loved him. He was honest, bright, warm and really great to be around. For quite a while, David, Angie, he and I would hang out together, but nothing ever stays the same. You want it to stay the same, but it never does.

I remember I took my only night off from 'Catch My Soul', which was a terrible, unprofessional thing to do, to go down to the Glastonbury Festival with the three of them and Bob Grace from Chrysalis. There was chaos over who was playing, David and Angie were there with their baggy trousers, it was a sunny day. Everyone was on acid, not David and Angie or De Fries I hasten to add, or even me for once. It was a great day and everyone was looning around, but they had a mix-up over who was going to appear on stage that evening, and David wasn't on until the next day and we had nowhere to sleep and we couldn't find a hotel room. Anyway, they

finally put David on stage, on his own with a guitar at 5am and he sang 'Memory of a Free Festival'. I think he sang something like, 'The sun machine is coming down, and we're gonna have a party, yeah, yeah, yeah.' And at that point, the sun broke over the hill top and hit the silver pyramid down in the valley. People were waking up in their sleeping bags having been frozen all night in the mud. It was quite extraordinary really, amazing, because he didn't have a full audience in attendance but the ones that he did have, he completely won over. I was up on the side of the stage and I watched it all. Later in the day, I went back to appear in 'Catch My Soul'.

After meeting De Fries, he asked me to get out of my old contract and said that he would look after me if I wanted, and as I so adored him it seemed like the best idea. So I willingly put my life, my time, my music and everything into his hands, a move which I don't ever regret. Around this time, I went for an audition for **Superstar** and got the part, and by this time I was already hanging out quite a lot with David and Ronno and Angie. **Superstar** came in the middle of it all, which was great because suddenly I was making good money, but under the deal which I had with Mainman, they took all the money and I was given a wage. By this time, I was given a really good wage. So I did **Superstar** for a year and a quarter and did the album at the same time. This was the 'Weren't Born a Man' album.

After **Superstar** finished I went to live in America because De Fries said that if you want to make it in the States, then you have to live there. It was certainly one of the best

117

educations that I have ever had. The first time that I was there, we stayed in places like the Sherry Netherland Hotel, and we would be out on the road looning about. Already Mainman had got all of these Warhol people on their staff which meant that Mainman had a great image over there.

I lived in New York for about two years and I regularly travelled out to see David perform at places like The O'Keefe Centre in Toronto, or I'd go to LA to see him at the Universal Amphitheatre for a week. So I was having a great time and would regularly venture back into the madness of living in the hotel, the Beverley Wiltshire in LA — where everything cost a fortune and drugs were everywhere. I mean, it was just a kind of madness, but it was a kind of constructive madness. I'll never say that it was bad.

It was great to see people like David and Marc Bolan hanging out all night. We would see the dawn come up loads of times. Or there would be David, Jagger and I plonking on the piano and basically just over-abusing all kinds of goodies, but trying to make some music and fool around. Everyone was trying to find themselves during that period.

It was around this time that my 'Ain't Gonna Play No Second Fiddle' album came out. A lot of people thought that I chose that title because I felt in the shadow of Bowie, which wasn't true. I knew always that De Fries had more time to spend for Bowie than for me because Bowie was much more ready than I was. In fact, I used that title because it was an old Bessie Smith song, and I'd always liked the lyrics. De Fries encouraged me to put a band together while in the States and so when David wasn't working, I would often use Earl Slick and Mike Kamen because they were on the Mainman payroll and needed to be used. By this time I had got my own apartment, which had been the Mainman offices but had been turned into an apartment for me to use on 58th street in between Second and Third. We took over the place from Leee Childers and Wayne County and I lived there for quite a long time. That was great because I actually got into being part of the American lifestyle by having my own place and not just being in the Sherry Netherlands and living off room service. I had to suddenly start cooking and going shopping, but living next to Bloomingdales with an account that Mainman paid for was a help of course!

In the middle of it all I would keep going off to Mustique because the guy that owned the island was a friend of mine — or I would sing at a party or something for Princess Margaret. I turned De Fries on to Mustique, he would go there with his girlfriend Melanie. It was while we were there one time that I heard about him being a bit dissatisfied with David. He wouldn't really talk about it but David had been calling and wanted to speak to him but he didn't want to speak to him. He just got on a plane for Mustique where no telephones can get through anyway. It was at this time that both David and De Fries decided that the split would happen. He didn't talk about it to me except to say that he couldn't handle David any more. But, it was while we were sitting in the sun in Mustique that it actually happened.

I flew back to London, leaving everything

♦ *New Year Oddity '79.*

in New York and never saw any of it again. While I was here the Mainman-David thing kind of collapsed. I was sort of put-out-to-grass, kept at bay in London. Everyone went into a kind of shock... we all treated each other in a way that you only do when you are hurt. David was only speaking to De Fries through lawyers and things between Angie and David were starting to collapse. De Fries did support me financially for another nine months or so until he said he was leaving the music business and he dropped out for a while. I didn't see too much of David during this time — I would see a lot of Angie as she was recovering from a broken heart. There was the house in Oakley Street and a lot of hanging out and looning went on there. It was a kind of a beginning of a downfall. For me, it left me very emotionally

crushed, more so about De Fries than about David because David is like me, he's a performer. You give your main thing to the public, you have to do that, you have to give everything because that's your main thing and so it is expected.

Because of this disaster, I saw very little of David, and also, because I was Angie's friend — and still am Angie's friend, I think the conflict between David and Angie made it much more difficult. Maybe Corinne also helped as well to keep Angie away from him which meant that communication was a bit down at that time.

It was such a shame because the company was so great, the offices were great, everything from T-shirts, stickers to Mainman newsletters — everything was so well done that it was suddenly sad that it all ended. It meant a great hardship for me because I had been on RCA during this period when the two albums came out. Suddenly I was without a record company, nobody to look after me and no one who could top De Fries in intelligence or deals or money making on my behalf. Plus, he wouldn't actually let me go unless somebody paid back all the money that he had spent on me, which was unthinkable because it was so much."

Without getting too technical about it, a fairly lengthy period of legal wrangling between Dana's legal-aid funded lawyers and Tony De Fries's lawyers prevailed throughout 1975/76, a time of great hardship for Dana who was desperately trying to escape her Mainman contract to enable herself to start earning again. Things changed for the better, when, in the middle of proceedings, De Fries telephoned Dana and invited her to L.A. to talk through the problem to hopefully solve it amicably. The rift was then closed almost completely and contact regularly maintained.

The one close friendship that has been maintained to this day, is Dana's friendship with Angie. Dana told me a little of the recent traumas that have hit Angie: "I still see a lot of Angie although she hasn't been back to London for quite a while. She rang me two or three months ago in tears saying her father had just died the night before. I said 'Oh god, how terrible for your mother, how is she taking it?', and she said, 'She died three months ago.' So I realised then how out-of-touch I had become. Angie and I will still send letters to each other, or pick up the telephone, but she has to normally ring me because she changes apartments so often.

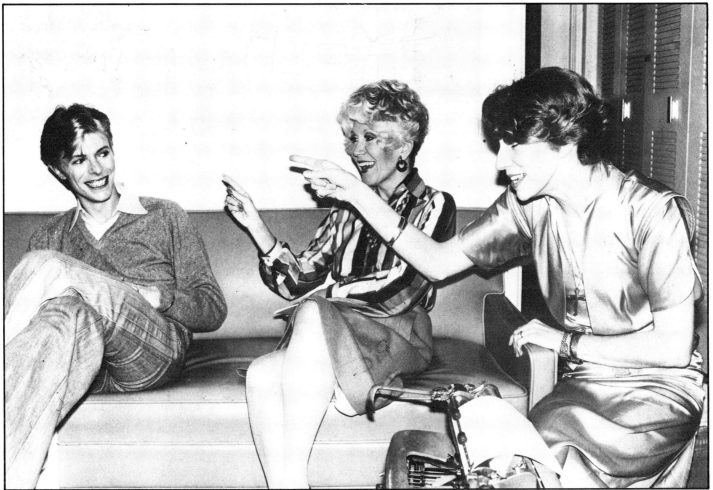

LFI

♦ *David with Angie on the Rena Barret Show, USA 1975.*

I haven't seen Zowie since he was about eleven I guess. I bet he's pretty amazing now".

I asked Dana about the early American experiences shared with David while on his Diamond Dogs jaunt. She immediately recalled a whole batch of memories as clear as if it was a tour in 1984, not of events a decade before..."It was the first time I ever saw somebody that I knew, really, really knew from the beginning, really hitting the big time in such a way that it was great fun. He had his Cadillac and if it wasn't me or Angie or Corinne travelling with him, he always had somebody with him while he travelled from gig to gig all night. Travelling like that or rehearsing in these huge aircraft hangars where he would be with the band and Toni Basil. I remember David was the first person that said, 'Listen, you've got to watch The Lockers, you've got to see Toni Basil's dancing.' I don't know if The Lockers were ever shown in this country, but they were the greatest dance group I've ever seen. I was very impressed with her and I really liked some of the things David was doing. For me,

the Diamond Dogs concerts were about the best concerts I had ever seen from any performer.

I saw every night at the Universal Amphitheatre, right at the front with Angie. She would cling hold of my arm at the important parts, especially when he would go out on the little chair which was the capsule thing for 'Space Oddity'. That was quite moving because there was always the worry that someone would stand on somebody else's shoulders and grab him from underneath. But, from the very first time that the metal box opened and he sat in this huge hand, the lighting was just brilliant, Jules Fischer was really a very good choice — a very expensive choice but a very good one all the same. It must be difficult for kids to have understood how he was then because there was so much ground that wasn't covered musically and image that hadn't been covered. He was exactly at the right place at the right time to create a new image when nobody had any answers. I mean, if you think of the lead singer of Duran Duran, the image is pathetic

compared to someone like Bowie... they're just not inventive enough. He came along at the time when there was a wide open space that could be filled, and he filled it absolutely right.

For me, if I say that Elvis was the greatest for the fifties and The Beatles for the sixties, I think that David was for the seventies. When I hear 'Let's Dance' I still think he's got it for the eighties, I still think he's really great. I'm not sure about the new album though, 'God Only Knows' sounds like Dudley Moore doing a piss take. Still, not everybody can turn out a great album for everybody's taste..."

There was a long period of time in 1975 when strange reports drifted across the Atlantic expressing concern for Bowie's well being. On-set reports from **The Man Who Fell To Earth** *in New Mexico were of a thin rock star avoiding sunlight, rarely eating and apparently locking himself away in his hotel room, practising the habitual pursuits of cocaine. Genuine worry spread through a tightly knit fan connection in the UK, eventually to the point when some London fans* *organised a petition and lobbied music newspapers and radio stations alike. London based Capital Radio took that worry seriously and helped garner counter claims from RCA that DB was well and happy and working hard etc. etc.... The truth, as has since been chronicled more than once by the man himself, is rather different and lays bare, the adage that unlimited drugs or any amount of drugs are wonderful even though they are part of the cool rewards of success. Why he decided to put himself through that sustained period of self abuse is unclear and has never been properly answered.*

That period was abruptly interrupted by Bowie himself through the action of one person, who had issued an ultimatum that he should clean-up, or she would go. Just why he had let himself get that far was unclear, but Dana put her angle on the situation.

"A lot of people kind of put down the use of coke, heavy abuse of, which in his case, of course, was very difficult. For a singer, your voice goes, and you forget a lot of things. But when you've got a fifty city tour, and you're absolutely knackered, unless you've already got your life-style and your ship together before you set off on this tour, it's hard to keep going. Very few people have actually got their lives organised when this fame hits you and you've got to have a couple of years of whooping it up to celebrate it in order to settle down. So I absolutely understand why he did what he did."

Did that worry you, because you were obviously around while all of this was going on?

"No, well I did quite a bit too. But it was never quite the same for me because it was never my glory, I was just part of the thing and having a good time. When I would hear from De Fries that he was complaining that he had no money, I would feel bad because Angie might have, for example, gone out and bought me 20 pairs of shoes, or been into Fredericks of Hollywood and bought me 30 pairs of French knickers or whatever. She would go and buy the clothes for everybody which was great because I hated shopping and David hated shopping, but she loved it."

And what about meeting David today?

"I don't know what...I think if I ran into David now, we would just look at each other and laugh because when you go through a lot when you are very young, things don't really change. Even when I knew him in my teenage years we might go through six months

♦ *Marvel-ous Team Up 1: Bowie and Ronson 1973.*

without any contact and then suddenly he would turn up on the doorstep. It never really made any difference, nothing changed. That's how friendships really survive in this business, you have to forget the difference between physical and mental time, it has to take on a new meaning. You have to realise that perhaps you won't see a person for a couple of years."

So when was the last time you saw him?

"It's a long time, I guess it would have been Marc's funeral. He sent his love to me a few months back, when he was down at Gaz's Monday night record hop, because my sax player was there and saw him. But I'm never around to see anyone, since 1980 I've been mostly out of England. I hear feedback about what is going on with the old team.

I used to have this very large flat in South Kensington and I used to have a lot of friends drop by to see me there. Somewhere I have a tape of David creating a song with Marc Bolan crashing about on some instruments which I used to have lying around. Because my home was so big and I was in a lot more than I am now, you could always be sure that a lot of people would always drop by. So it would turn into a big social gathering, and David would often drop by and Marc too. It was a rare old time."

Time was a rare commodity here too and before we knew it, it was time to finish. As we walked off towards the tube, more little bits of the past suddenly sprang to Dana's mind, "You know, David had this curious problem with his back which used to cause him all kinds of trouble and there was...oh, this is where I have to go. We'll have to finish this another time."   ●

♦ *Marvel-ous Team Up 2: Bowie and Iggy 1977.*

Ira Cohen

National Film Archives

Just for the record..

David Bowie has always wrenched opinions on himself from the broadest cross-section of famous and infamous people. This section is comprised of a balanced selection of just some of those quotes...

"I'm a fan of songs rather than people. For instance, David Bowie's written a couple of good tunes, but really, I think he's a bit of an idiot."
Alexei Sayle (1983)

"I don't want to know about Bowie any more. I hear he went around on the last tour like a tramp, then put on his blonde wig and suit and went on-stage."
Phil Oakey (1983)

"I've seen David Bowie. He needs mothering."
Tom Jones (1975)

"David's a brilliant guy – the painting, the writing. He's a very generous kid. Very shy, but with me he can be himself. I'm like his father."
Tony Masicia, bodyguard (1978)

"He sings a lovely counterpoint."
Bing Crosby (1977)

"I met Bowie at an Iggy Pop gig. I thought he was Iggy's manager or something. 'Hunky Dory' was OK but he's just a prat really. He got into believing his own publicity. 'Oh, I'm a man of many parts'. He can't act either."
Johnny Rotten (1978)

"Never wear a new pair of shoes in front of him."
Mick Jagger (1980)

"Bowie is one of the few originals. He has a great sense of theatre and is one of the few people I respect in this business. Bowie, Elton and I are very competitive. I see what they do and I say 'I can do better than that' and when I do, I want them to say 'I can do better than that' and when they do I go one step further. That keeps everything healthy and interesting. They represent showbiz and I respect them for that."
Alice Cooper (1974)

"I would walk out of a room to avoid him."
Rod Stewart (1983)

"This intelligent, very sensitive fellow who came from the same part of London as Charlie, walked in and wanted to talk. I really am very fond of him."
Oona Chaplin (1981)

"I thank God David is English."
Nile Rodgers (1983)

"People say I'm a Ziggy clone, but I never even saw Ziggy!"
Peter Murphy (1982)

"When Bowie came to see us in PORK with his floppy hat and dress, Leee Black Childers, who was also working for Alice Cooper, told Bowie that Alice was happening in the States and that he should present himself in some way. Before you know it, Bowie told everyone he was gay."
Jayne County (1977)

"Outsiders think of him as feminine but he's the exact opposite."
Ava Cherry (1983)

"Can't fucking act, can ya."
Tim Butler of the Psychedelic Furs (1977)

"What's Bowie got to do with me? He's 33 and I'm 21."
Tony Hadley (1980)

"We are distant friends, although I dream about him a lot."
Hazel O'Connor (1981)

"Imagine being kissed by David Bowie!!"
Roberta Flack (1975)

"I'm interested in what Bowie does because I care about what he does."
David Sylvian (1982)

"He's simply charming."
Geraldine Chaplin (1981)

"When we were recording 'Under Pressure', to have his ego involved with ours was a very

◆ *Preparing to 'Duke' it out.*

volatile mixture. It made for a hot time in the studio."
Brian May (1981)

"He keeps changing. He won't get old like the others."
Siouxsie (1976)

"He's pretty good for 36 or 38 or whatever he is."
Bruce Watson of Big Country (1983)

♦ Arriving at Sadlers Wells, London March 1982. Long time minder, Tony Mascia, following closely behind.

Larry Bulaitis

"He's fantastic!"
Elizabeth Taylor (1974)

"A lot of people want to be like David Bowie. I don't. I think he's had it really. I think he's great, brilliant but he's just there like Harrods or Frank Sinatra."
Boy George(1981)

"It's great – Do you have any other records of interest?"
John Lennon to Bowie on hearing 'Young Americans' (1975)

"He has one of the most outstanding faces of the 20th Century."
Mac McCulloch (1983)

"His voice doesn't speak to me. I don't like that kind of whining sound."
Stewart Copeland of the Police (1983)

"If you listen to the new wave stuff, you can see and hear the influences. It's all Bowie and Roxy."
Paul McCartney(1979)

"Bowie and I got married, then we split up around 1973 . . . no really, we were never enemies. The press made all that up. They did it with Bowie and Bolan but those guys were good friends. Same with Lennon and McCartney."
Alice Cooper(1982)

"I was upstairs at the Embassy Club in Bond Street when I spotted Bowie. Naturally, I went over and sat on his lap. Imagine my surprise when he turned around, grabbed me and started sucking my neck. He was a bit forward I thought so I pushed him off. But it was not before he'd managed to plant a big

red love-bite all over me."
Marilyn (1983)

"David Bowie met people who made him weird. I was born weird."
Boy George (1980)

"Marc Bolan was the first with the glam bit. That's not a downer on David, it's just that I think Marc was the first original."
Ringo Starr (1983)

"What's this? Are you disguised as Angie Bowie tonight?"
Flo and Eddie on Alice Cooper's dress sense (1980)

"Bowie was good for a while but you couldn't really get into it 'cause you didn't believe that he was doing what he believed in. He was like a really bad drag queen. Bad stuff. 'Rebel

124

Rebel' was a good single. It's about the New York Dolls I think."
Johnny Rotten (1977)

Tom and Barbara Good on do-it-yourself haircuts:
Tom: "How about a David Bowie?"
Barbara runs away . . .
'The Good Life' BBC TV (1976)

"When I started 'The Man Who Fell to Earth' with David, people came up to me and said – 'It's a great idea, but can he act'. I said 'Well, what do you think he does in front of ten thousand people at the Hollywood Bowl – That isn't him!"
Nicolas Roeg (1983)

"He's a messy kisser. His tongue is everywhere. You feel like he's trying to wash your teeth."
Candy Clark (1975)

"When we first met David he thought we were really heavy people and he was shaking."
Ian Hunter (1981)

"He was one of the first to be theatrical in his show."
Klaus Nomi (1980)

"I had to do more homework with him than with anyone else. He's an extraordinary talent who has his hand in everything."
Toni Basil (1982)

"David is this strange, androgynous character."
Tony Scott (1983)

"David always likes to get in dresses if possible."
Mick Jagger (1985)

"David is my favourite singer next to my Mum and Dad. And you know, I like him better than Michael Jackson. Sorry Michael."
Sean Lennon (1984)

"A man of few words . . ."
Lulu (1981)

"A man of few words but a lot of talent."
Dave Lee Travis (1 second after)

"There is the sense, when you are working with him, that he is the only thing happening, that he is it."
Michael Kamen (1974)

"Titanically talented."
Stan Lee (1975)

"David's an innovator. He started things and set trends for groups that hadn't even been thought of."
Johnny Carson (1980)

"David who?"
Starzone (1985) ●

125

RCA

Lastword...

And so it ends, this collection of anecdotes, facts and trivia. Some notables boasting strong connections with the Bowie myth managed to escape our net. Not neglecting the project for any reason other than our paths never quite managed to cross.

Despite that, we feel that those people we did talk to offer a fair section of the many different and often equally talented individuals that contributed so much to David Bowie's career.

Without them, the story would be nowhere near as glamorous....

For information about 'Starzone' magazine and its David Bowie Fan Club services, plus any comments or correspondence on this book, write to: David Currie, Starzone, PO Box 225, Watford, Herts, WD1 7QG, England. Please enclose an SAE when enquiring about the fan club.